WONKY
One-Block
Quilts

Simple Technique, Dramatic Results

Marlous Carter

C&T PUBLISHING

Text copyright © 2011 by Marlous Carter

Artwork copyright © 2011 by C&T Publishing, Inc.

Publisher: Amy Marson

Creative Director: Gailen Runge

Acquisitions Editor: Susanne Woods

Editor: Liz Aneloski

Technical Editors: Teresa Stroin and Gailen Runge

Cover Designer: Kristy Zacharias

Book Designer: Christina D. Jarumay

Production Coordinator: Jenny Leicester

Production Editor: Alice Mace Nakanishi

Illustrator: Wendy Mathson

Photography by Christina Carty-Francis and Diane Pedersen of C&T Publishing, Inc., unless otherwise noted

Published by C&T Publishing, Inc., P.O. Box 1456, Lafayette, CA 94549

Library of Congress Cataloging-in-Publication Data

Carter, Marlous, 1960-

 Wonky one-block quilts : simple technique, dramatic results / Marlous Carter.

   p. cm.

 ISBN 978-1-60705-201-2 (softcover)

 1. Quilting. 2. Patchwork quilts. I. Title.

 TT835.C386 2011

 746.46--dc22

                              2010033969

Printed in China

10 9 8 7 6 5 4 3 2 1

DEDICATION

Judy Hugo, friend and silent partner (well, not so silent!), has, over time, evolved from friend to proofreader/editor, pattern tester, and overall cheerleader. I could not do this without her.

ACKNOWLEDGMENTS

Karen Gibbs, friend and longarm quilter extraordinaire, who always makes my quilts look fantastic

Nancy Frank, whose longarm quilting hobby has grown into so much more

Diana Marshall of the Gloversville Sewing Center, a most understanding and supportive boss

Linda Fieldhouse, Linda Noto, and Claudia Collins, binding fairies spectaculaire

Liz Aneloski and the rest of the knowledgeable and friendly staff at C&T Publishing, who did not mind holding my hand and guiding me through the exciting process of authorship

Contents

Introduction

I absolutely love this wonky technique because it adds a layer of interest to any quilt block. Movement, visual interest, and unique block settings always catch my attention when I'm walking through a quilt show. With the wonky technique, my old favorites get a face-lift. No matter what traditional block I begin with, as soon as I've wonky cut the blocks and put them together, something new and wonderful emerges. The quilt has attitude—and who wouldn't like a little attitude in their quilts? After the block is wonky cut, the rigid lines, so familiar in traditional quilts with traditional settings, give way to an appearance of movement. The possibilities are endless—you can add the wonky technique to any traditional block you love.

WONKY FOUR-PATCH

Just look at what happens to a traditional Four-Patch!

Traditional Four-Patch setting

Wonky-cut Four-Patch

No special templates, rulers, or gadgets are needed for this technique. With your trusty 12½″ × 12½″ acrylic ruler and a rotary cutter (with a new blade, of course), you are on your way to a successful wonky experience.

I like to vary the style of quilts I do. Sometimes I want the simplicity of having to choose only four or five fabrics. Other times I like the challenge of having to choose 20 fat quarters. And then there are the times I like to just grab a 2½″ prepackaged strip bundle and go to town.

The eight projects in this book cover a wide range of tastes and styles—so there should be something for everyone. And all the projects have directions for various sizes.

The first chapter contains some basic tips and suggestions. The second chapter describes the wonky technique—you'll be surprised at its simplicity. Step 1 is squaring the blocks so that they truly are all the same size. This is absolutely necessary for the wonky cut to be a success. Then, with a twist of the ruler, you slice away—and presto, a block with attitude!

The first project is what I like to think of as a tutorial. Its basis is the Four Patch block; easy to piece, easy to wonky cut, and easy to construct. The bonus is that even though it is simple, the finished quilt looks intricate and eye-catching. By wonky cutting this simple, traditional block, you can see how stress-free it is to add new appeal to a traditional block. The steps in the wonky technique are the same no matter which traditional block you choose and no matter what size you need. That's what makes this technique so much fun.

A variety of border styles are presented in Bodacious Border Techniques and Options. Borders are an integral part of the overall design of a quilt. For this reason, you are given a selection of options: traditional single-fabric strips, pieced strips, crazy piecing, and raw-edge appliqué. And you can even use your leftovers for some of the border options.

Choose a project and enter the world of wonky cutting. You will never look at a block the same way again!

FYI

Before we get to the heart of this book, I'd like to share some basic stuff I've discovered over the years.

FABRIC

Fabric is candy for quilters; it is our passion, our obsession, our addiction. We spend countless hours at the local quilt shop as we agonize over the perfect fabric grouping for the next project. Choosing fabric for a quilt can be challenging, as we put a little of ourselves in each quilt we make. For this reason, the fabrics you choose have to be perfect—*for you* and *only you!*

There really isn't any right or wrong fabric choice, and lessons will be learned with each quilt you make. However, here are some steps to follow:

1. Pick a fabric you absolutely love, and then add more fabrics. Include a variety of textures and colors.

2. Arrange the fabrics so you see only a little of each, and place a background fabric across them, so you can see what the background looks like alongside each of the other fabrics.

3. Stand back 4–5 feet. Remove any fabrics that blend too much with the background.

4. Is there a "bully" in the group—a fabric that constantly draws your eye away from all the rest? If so, add another of similar intensity or eliminate it all together.

5. Make sure you have enough variety. The entire group should be interesting when seen from a distance and have some fun visual details when viewed up close.

PROJECT TIPS AND NOTES

- Read through the instructions for the entire project before you make your first cut.

- Yardage requirements given are ample and should include enough fabric for shrinkage and straightening. The requirements are based on a usable 42″ strip once the selvages have been sparingly trimmed.

- Batting and backing requirements are 4″ larger all around than the finished size of the quilt.

- All yardages for binding are based on 2½″-wide strips, cut selvage to selvage. If you prefer your binding to be cut on the bias, add ¼–⅓ yard to the total fabric requirement for binding.

- Initial cuts for all the projects are given widthwise (selvage to selvage).

- The projects include multiple size options. Mark with a highlighter the directions for the size you are making. This will lessen the chance of cutting the wrong size.

- I have discovered that a scant ¼″ seam works much better in achieving the correct overall block size. What I mean by a scant ¼″ is that the seam is one thread of fabric less than the full ¼″ seam. Therefore, I set my needle position one setting over to the right.

- Always press the fabric after every step.

- Before you begin any project, please review the instructions for the wonky technique (pages 9–12).

BACKING

To determine the batting and backing size, measure the length and width of the finished quilt top and add 8″.

If the quilt backing is no more than 82″ long, the back will have one horizontal seam.

If the quilt backing is more than 82″ long but less than 82″ wide, it will have one vertical seam.

If the quilt backing is more than 82″ long and more than 82″ wide, it will have two horizontal seams.

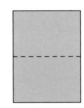

No more than 82″ long

More than 82″ long but less than 82″ wide

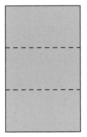

More than 82″ long and more than 82″ wide

✳ TIP

Most quilt shops now carry a variety of extra-wide backing fabrics that range from 60″ to 108″ wide or wider. These save time and often money, and I must admit I look there first when looking for backing fabric.

BINDING

✖ note

I usually trim and square my quilts before attaching the binding. Even if a quilt top is square when I send it to my friend and quilter, Karen, to be quilted, it is not always so when it returns—this is just the nature of the beast when quilting.

Using a 16″ or 8½″ × 24″ ruler, I trim the excess batting and backing and make the corners square.

How Much?

1. Measure all 4 sides of the quilt.

2. Add these measurements together and add 10″ for folding and seams. You now have the total length needed to go around the quilt.

3. Divide this number by 40 and round up. This will give you the number of strips you need to sew end to end. (I don't usually miter my seams when making the binding.) Now you know how many strips you will need to cut.

✖ note

Example

Quilt measures 64″ × 84″.

Add all 4 sides plus 10″ = 306″.

Divide 306″ by 40″ = 7.65; you will need to cut 8 strips.

I cut my binding strips 2½″ wide across the grain (selvage to selvage).

Preparing and Sewing the Binding

1. Sew the strips together end to end, trim one end at a 45° angle, and press ¼″ of the trimmed end to the wrong side.

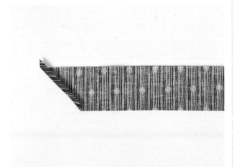

2. Press the entire binding in half lengthwise, wrong sides together.

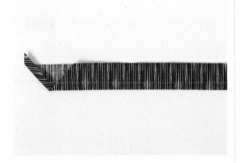

3. Working on the right side of the quilt, sew the binding on with the raw edges aligned, using a ¼″ seam and a walking foot.

4. Begin stitching at the end of the binding, stop when you come to the pressed-under fold, and begin again about 1½″ past the fold. This leaves a space for tucking in the other end once you have sewn all the way around.

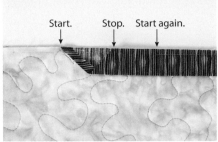

Start.   Stop.   Start again.

5. Stop ¼″ from the corner and backstitch.

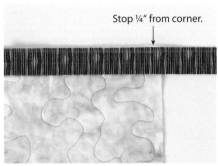

Stop ¼″ from corner.

6. Remove the quilt from the sewing machine.

7. Turn the quilt; fold the binding up and then down alongside the next edge of the quilt.

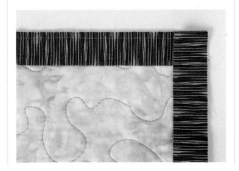

8. Stitch along the next edge of the quilt until you reach ¼″ from the next corner. Repeat Steps 5–7 for this corner and for all subsequent corners.

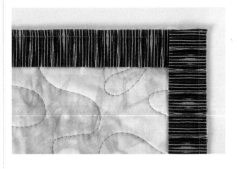

9. When you reach the beginning again, cut the end of the binding at an angle and tuck it into the beginning section of the binding. Continue stitching until you are stitching over what is already stitched; then backstitch, and you're done.

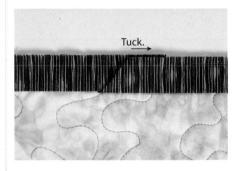

Tuck.

10. Press the binding to the back and hand stitch in place.

CUTTING BASICS

Straightening the Fabric

In order for cutting and subsequent piecing to go smoothly, first you will need to straighten—or, in quilting lingo, to "square"—the fabric.

1. Iron out all the wrinkles and fold the fabric selvage to selvage.

2. With the selvages aligned, hold the fabric up so that the fold hangs down.

3. Look at how the fabric hangs. Is it nice and straight, or is it wavy and lumpy? If it's wavy and lumpy, shift one of the selvage edges to the left or right (but keep it lined up with the other selvage edge) until the fabric hangs down smoothly.

4. Place the folded fabric on the cutting mat with the fold toward you and the edge you are going to cut to the right. (If you are left-handed, you will place the edge to cut on the left.)

5. Choose an acrylic ruler that is long enough to reach from fold to selvage. Working on the right edge (if you are left-handed you will work on the left edge), align a horizontal line on the ruler with the folded edge. Be sure the ruler extends farther than the selvages.

6. Slide the ruler as close to the right edge (or to the left edge, if left-handed) of the fabric as you can while keeping 2 layers of fabric under the ruler. As you slide the ruler over, keep the ruler line aligned on the fold.

7. Press firmly on the ruler and cut along the edge of the ruler using a rotary cutter. Always cut away from yourself.

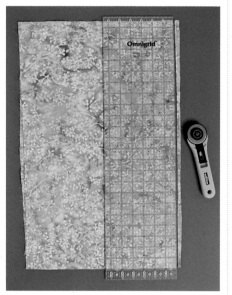

Cut to square fabric.

Cutting

❈ *note*

The process for trimming selvages is the same as for squaring the fabric.

1. After the fabric has been straightened, carefully pinch the corners and flip the fabric so the straightened edge is to the left (or to the right, if left-handed) and the fold is still toward you. When doing this "flip" it is important to keep the cut edge and the selvages lined up.

2. Place a ruler next to the selvages and cut along the edge of the ruler using a rotary cutter.

❈ *note*

When cutting strips, place the ruler on the left side. (If you are left-handed, you will place the ruler on the right side.)

3. To cut strips, align a horizontal line on the ruler with the folded edge. As an example, if you need to cut a strip 4½˝ wide, line up the 4½˝ line of the ruler on the squared edge of the fabric and cut with the rotary cutter.

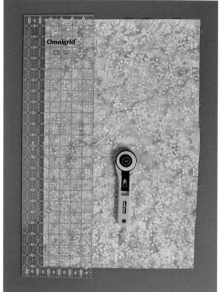

Cut 4½˝ strip.

The Wonky Technique

SQUARING

⊞ *note*

For the wonky technique you must start with blocks that are all exactly the same size. For this reason it is important to trim the blocks down to the size required for the quilt you are making.

Most of the quilts in this book begin with a 12½″ × 12½″ pieced block that is trimmed down to 12″ × 12″. Whatever the size of the block you need, the steps for trimming it down to a particular size are the same.

It is important to measure from the center of the block so all the seams are in the same position for each block.

Block center

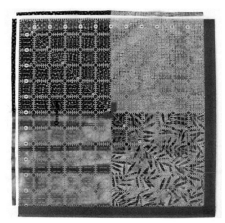

Left-handed

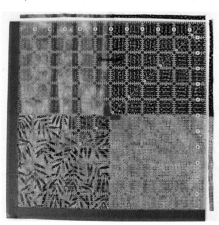

Right-handed

Center measured square over center of block and trim.

Block with a Center Seam

1. Using painter's tape, mark the acrylic ruler with the block size you are trimming to and mark the center of that block. We are trimming to 12″ × 12″, so mark the 12″ × 12″ square and the center point, which is 6″ from the edge.

2. Place the ruler with the center of the 12″ × 12″ marked square over the center of the block and trim the right and top edges of the block (left and top if you are left-handed).

3. Rotate the block so the trimmed corner is now the bottom left corner (bottom right for left-handers).

4. Place the acrylic ruler so that the lines of the 12″ × 12″ square lie on the left and bottom edges of the block (right and bottom for left-handers) and the center is over the center of the block. Trim the right and top edges of the block (left and top for left-handers).

The block is now trimmed down to 12″ × 12″.

Squared block

Block without a Center Seam

1. To find the center of a block that does not have a center seam, measure ¼ of it and mark the block at the corner of the acrylic square—I usually use a flower-head pin.

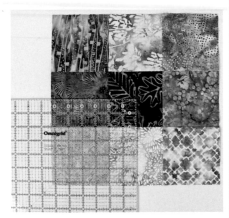

Flower-head pin indicates center of block.

2. If the block measures 12½″ × 12½″, place the ruler marks for a 6¼″ square on the lower left quadrant and place a flower-head pin at the tip of the right corner. Now you know where the center is. Trim as shown in Steps 2–4 in Block with a Center Seam (page 9).

✳ TIP

Flower-head pins allow the ruler to lie flat when placed on top.

THE WONKY CUT

✽ note

For most of the patterns in this book, you will begin with a 12½″ × 12½″ block that you trim down to 12″ × 12″ before beginning the wonky cut (see Squaring, page 9).

General Instructions

1. With blue painter's tape, mark a 10½″ × 10½″ square on your 12½″ × 12½″ square acrylic ruler. This will be the guide for the size of square you will trim down to using the wonky technique.

2. Divide the blocks into 2 piles; label one pile A and the other pile B.

3. Follow the directions carefully for the quilt you are making and always check the angle of the ruler for both A and B blocks.

Pile A

It is very important to keep the angle of the ruler the same each time you begin the wonky cut and to make sure the angle is correct for the block you are cutting. Look closely at the instructions for the quilt you are making to see which are A and which are B blocks. *A blocks always have the ruler angled in one direction, and B blocks have the ruler angled in the other direction.*

1. Place your square ruler as shown, so the corners of the marked 10½″ × 10½″ square touch each edge of the pieced block and the center of the square (5¼″) is over the center of the pieced block. The center is easy to find with the Four Patch block.

2. Trim.

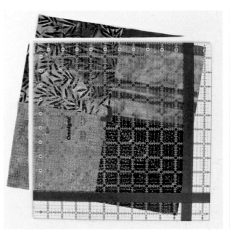

Left-handed   Right-handed

Orient ruler and trim.

3. Rotate the block as shown and place the ruler on the block, lining up the edges of the marked 10½″ × 10½″ square. Trim to measure 10½″ × 10½″.

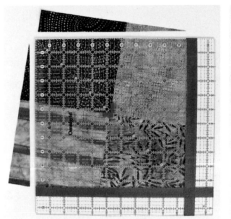

Left-handed

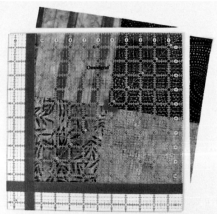

Right-handed

Orient ruler and trim.

4. Trim all the A blocks in the same manner, being sure to start with the same ruler angle across the top each time.

Block A

Pile B

1. Place your square ruler as shown, so that the corners of the marked 10½″ × 10½″ square touch each edge of the pieced block and the center of the square (5¼″) is over the center of the pieced block.

2. Trim.

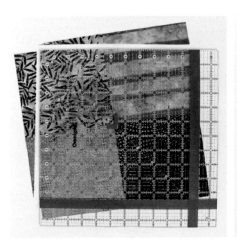

Left-handed

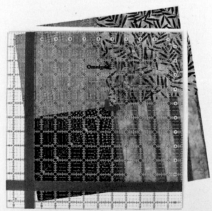

Right-handed

Orient ruler and trim.

3. Rotate the block as shown and place the ruler on the block, lining up the edges of the marked 10½″ × 10½″ square. Trim to measure 10½″ × 10½″.

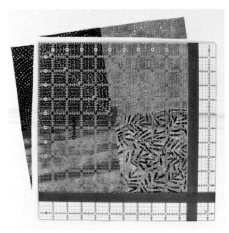

Left-handed

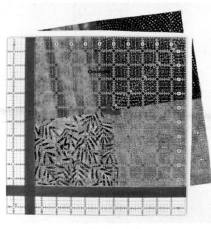

Right-handed

Orient ruler and trim.

4. Trim all the B blocks in the same manner, being sure to start with the same ruler angle across the top each time.

Block B

Block A

Block B

⊞ *note*

If you are working with a block that doesn't have a seam to indicate the center, mark the center with a flower pin, as you did when squaring (page 9), and then follow the wonky cut steps given for Blocks A and B (pages 10–12).

Stepping Stones
WONKY TECHNIQUE TUTORIAL

64" × 84"
Quilt made by Marlous Carter
and quilted by Karen Gibbs.
Border 2 uses options 3 and 4
(pages 62 and 63).

■ **Finished Four Patch block size:** 10" × 10"

*The Four-Patch is a very simple block to piece and a great one for
learning the wonky technique. This quilt uses only four different
fabrics and goes together quickly.*

MATERIALS

	CRIB 44″ × 54″	LAP 55″ × 74″	TWIN 64″ × 84″	QUEEN 88″ × 108″	KING 108″ × 108″
Blocks: 4 fabrics*	½ yard of each fabric	⅞ yard of each fabric	⅞ yard of each fabric	1⅝ yards of each fabric	2⅛ yards of each fabric
Borders 1 and 3	½ yard	½ yard	⅞ yard	1 yard	1⅛ yards
Border 2**	⅜ yard	⅜ yard	¾ yard	⅞ yard	1 yard
Border 4	⅝ yard	1¼ yards	1½ yards	2½ yards	2¾ yards
Backing	3 yards	3⅝ yards	5¼ yards	8¼ yards	10 yards
Binding	½ yard	⅝ yard	⅝ yard	⅞ yard	1 yard

*4 contrasting fabrics: 2 light/medium values and 2 dark values (can also contrast texture or print)

**Yardage is given without using scraps. See complete border instructions for all sizes (pages 17 and 18).

CUTTING INSTRUCTIONS

	CRIB	LAP	TWIN	QUEEN	KING
Blocks: from each fabric*	2 strips 6½″ × wof**	4 strips 6½″ × wof**	4 strips 6½″ × wof**	10 strips 6½″ × wof**	11 strips 6½″ × wof**
Borders 1 and 3	8 strips 1½″ × wof	7 strips 2″ × wof	12 strips 2″ × wof	16 strips 2″ × wof	18 strips 2″ × wof
Border 2	4 strips 2½″ × wof	3 strips 3½″ × wof	6 strips 3½″ × wof	8 strips 3½″ × wof	9 strips 3½″ × wof
Border 4	5 strips 3½″ × wof	6 strips 6½″ × wof	7 strips 6½″ × wof	10 strips 8½″ × wof	11 strips 8½″ × wof

*Keep the strips cut from each fabric in a separate pile. You will have four piles.

**wof = width of fabric

PIECING THE BLOCKS

Use ¼″ seam allowances.

1. Pair the block fabric strips, 1 light/medium with 1 dark. Keep the pairing the same for each strip set.

2. Sew each pair of strips together. Press toward the dark fabric.

Make the following number of strip sets:
Crib: 2   Lap: 4   Twin: 4   Queen: 8   King: 11

Make the following number of strip sets:
Crib: 2   Lap: 4   Twin: 4   Queen: 8   King: 11

3. From each strip set, cut 6 rectangles 6½″ × 12½″ and set the remaining scrap aside for possible use in Border 2.

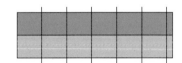

Cut 6 rectangles 6½″ × 12½″ from each strip set.

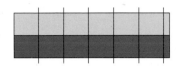

Cut 6 rectangles 6½″ × 12½″ from each strip set.

4. Place the rectangles in 2 piles, a pile for each fabric pair.

5. Take 1 rectangle from each pile and place the 2 rectangles right sides together, matching the center seams.

When placing the fabric units together, be sure the seam allowances lie in opposite directions so that you can "hook" or "nest" the seams together.

6. Sew all the blocks with the fabrics in exactly the same orientation.

7. Check to make sure the blocks all measure 12½″ × 12½″.

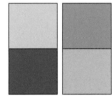

When placing units together, be sure that dark fabrics are diagonally across from each other and light fabrics are diagonally across from each other. All blocks must be exactly the same.

8. Make the following number of blocks:

Crib: 12   Lap: 20   Twin: 24   Queen: 48   King: 64.

Now it's time to give the blocks some attitude. Are you ready to wonk?

TRIMMING THE BLOCKS

See complete squaring and wonky technique instructions (pages 9–12).

1. Using the center of each block for orientation, square the blocks to measure 12″ × 12″ (see Squaring, page 9).

2. Divide the blocks into 2 equal piles and label them A and B.

Block A

> ⊞ *note*
>
> For the A and B piles in this quilt, the blocks are the same. However, the angle of the ruler will change from Block A to Block B. Be sure the ruler is angled correctly across the top every time you begin the wonky cut.

1. Place the marked square ruler at an angle on the block, so that the corners of the 10½″ × 10½″ marked square touch each edge of the block and the center of the marked square (5¼″) is directly over the center seam. Trim (page 10).

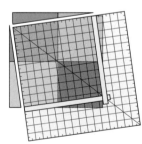 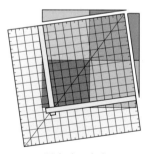

Left-handed   Right-handed

Correct ruler angle for first 2 cuts of Block A

2. Rotate the block and square the other 2 sides of the block to measure 10½″ × 10½″ (page 11).

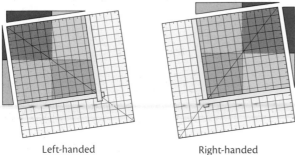

Left-handed   Right-handed
Correct ruler angle for last 2 cuts of Block A

3. Trim all the A blocks in the same way, with the ruler angle across the top the same every time you make the first wonky cut.

4. Make the following number of blocks:

Crib: 6   Lap: 10   Twin: 12   Queen: 24   King: 32

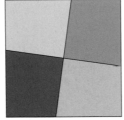

Block A

✳ TIP

Those funny pointy scraps that are left over after you've trimmed the blocks can be used in an optional technique for Border 2 (page 63), so don't throw them away.

Block B

1. Place the marked square ruler at an angle, so that the corners of the 10½″ × 10½″ marked square touch each edge of the block and the center of the square (5¼″ mark) is directly over the center seam (page 11). Notice the difference from the angle of Block A. Trim.

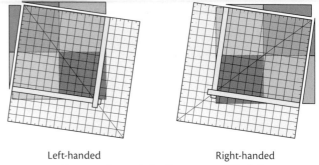

Left-handed   Right-handed
Correct ruler angle for first 2 cuts of Block B

2. Rotate the block and square the other 2 sides of the block to measure 10½″ × 10½″ (page 12).

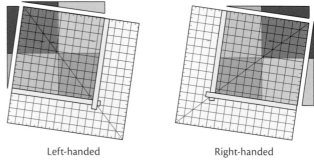

Left-handed   Right-handed
Correct ruler angle for last 2 cuts of Block B

3. Trim all the B blocks in the same way, with the ruler angle across the top the same every time you make the first wonky cut.

4. Make the following number of blocks:

Crib: 6   Lap: 10   Twin: 12   Queen: 24   King: 32

Block B

QUILT CONSTRUCTION

1. Place the blocks on a design wall or the floor (a favorite of mine!), alternating Blocks A and B.

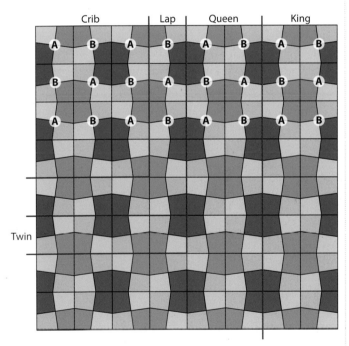

2. Sew the blocks into rows, alternating the pressing direction of the seams. Press the seams to the right in the first row, to the left in the second row, to the right in the third row, and so on.

3. Sew the rows together, matching the seams.

> ⊞ *note*
>
> *As an option, have some fun and play with the block placement.*
>
> *Leave all the A blocks as shown and rotate the B blocks.*
>
> *Or, leave all the B blocks and rotate the A blocks.*
>
> *Or, rotate the blocks until you get another design you like.*

BORDERS

It's time to grab those border strips we cut earlier.

This quilt has 4 borders. Border 2 has several options; choose which option you like best from Options for Border 2 (pages 61–63).

See General Border Instructions (page 60) to measure correct border lengths. None of us sews an exact ¼″ seam. Some of us sew a generous ¼″, and yet our quilt tops are smaller than the quilt tops of those of us who sew scant ¼″ seams. For this reason it is always a good idea to measure your quilt to get the correct border strip length needed every time you add a border.

See Bodacious Border Techniques and Options (pages 60–63) for complete sewing instructions for all borders.

	CRIB	LAP	TWIN	QUEEN	KING
Border 1	2 strips 1½″ × 30½″ 2 strips 1½″ × 42½″	2 strips 2″ × 40½″ 2 strips 2″ × 62½″	2 strips 2″ × 40½″ 2 strips 2″ × 63½″	2 strips 2″ × 60½″ 2 strips 2″ × 83½″	2 strips 2″ × 80½″ 2 strips 2″ × 83½″
Border 2	2 strips 2½″ × 32½″ 2 strips 2½″ × 46½″	2 strips 3½″ × 40½″ (top and bottom only)	2 strips 3½″ × 43½″ 2 strips 3½″ × 69½″	2 strips 3½″ × 63½″ 2 strips 3½″ × 89½″	2 strips 3½″ × 83½″ 2 strips 3½″ × 89½″
Border 3	2 strips 1½″ × 36½″ 2 strips 1½″ × 48½″	2 strips 2″ × 40½″ (top and bottom only)	2 strips 2″ × 49½″ 2 strips 2″ × 72½″	2 strips 2″ × 69½″ 2 strips 2″ × 92½″	2 strips 2″ × 89½″ 2 strips 2″ × 92½″
Border 4	2 strips 3½″ × 38½″ 2 strips 3½″ × 54½″	2 strips 6½″ × 43½″ 2 strips 6½″ × 74½″	2 strips 6½″ × 52½″ 2 strips 6½″ × 84½″	2 strips 8½″ × 72½″ 2 strips 8½″ × 108½″	2 strips 8½″ × 92½″ 2 strips 8½″ × 108½″

Stepping Stones II, 64″ × 84″
Quilt made by Judy Hugo
and quilted by Karen Gibbs.
Border 2 uses options 2, 3, and 4 (pages 62 and 63).

Zensational
2 BY 2 BLOCK

64" × 84"
Quilt made by Marlous Carter
and quilted by Karen Gibbs.
Border 2 uses option 3
(page 62).

■ **Finished 2 by 2 block size: 10" × 10"**

The 2 by 2 block is another super-easy block to piece and, when wonky cut, gives a really great sense of movement and interest. This quilt uses four different main fabrics plus a background fabric.

MATERIALS

	CRIB 44″ × 54″	LAP 55″ × 74″	TWIN 64″ × 84″	QUEEN 88″ × 108″	KING 108″ × 108″
Blocks: 4 fabrics	⅓ yard of each fabric	½ yard of each fabric	½ yard of each fabric	⅞ yard of each fabric	1¼ yards of each fabric
Background	⅞ yard	1⅔ yards	1⅔ yards	3¼ yards	4⅜ yards
Borders 1 and 3	½ yard	½ yard	⅞ yard	1 yard	1⅛ yards
Border 2*	⅜ yard	⅜ yard	¾ yard	⅞ yard	1 yard
Border 4	⅝ yard	1¼ yards	1½ yards	2½ yards	2¾ yards
Backing	3 yards	3⅝ yards	5¼ yards	8¼ yards	10 yards
Binding	½ yard	⅝ yard	⅝ yard	⅞ yard	1 yard

*Yardage is given without using scraps. See complete border instructions for all sizes (pages 23 and 24).

CUTTING INSTRUCTIONS

	CRIB	LAP	TWIN	QUEEN	KING
Blocks: from each fabric	2 strips 3½″ × wof*	4 strips 3½″ × wof*	4 strips 3½″ × wof*	8 strips 3½″ × wof*	11 strips 3½″ × wof*
Background	8 strips 3½″ × wof	16 strips 3½″ × wof	16 strips 3½″ × wof	32 strips 3½″ × wof	44 strips 3½″ × wof
Borders 1 and 3	8 strips 1½″ × wof	7 strips 2″ × wof	12 strips 2″ × wof	16 strips 2″ × wof	18 strips 2″ × wof
Border 2	4 strips 2½″ × wof	3 strips 3½″ × wof	6 strips 3½″ × wof	8 strips 3½″ × wof	9 strips 3½″ × wof
Border 4	5 strips 3½″ × wof	6 strips 6½″ × wof	7 strips 6½″ × wof	10 strips 8½″ × wof	11 strips 8½″ × wof

*wof = width of fabric

PIECING THE BLOCKS

Use ¼″ seam allowances.

1. Separate the 4 block fabric strips into 4 piles, with each pile having the same fabric. There will be piles A, B, C, and D.

2. Pair up each strip in each pile with a background strip.

3. Sew the strip pairs together and press toward the background fabric. Each pile should have the following number of strip sets:

Crib: 2   Lap: 4   Twin: 4
Queen: 8   King: 11

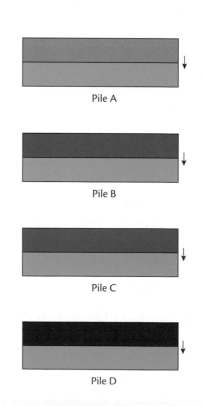

Pile A

Pile B

Pile C

Pile D

4. From each strip set, cut 6 squares 6½″ × 6½″. Divide the squares cut from each pile into 2 equal piles. You will have 2 A piles, 2 B piles, 2 C piles, and 2 D piles.

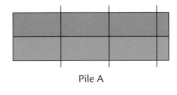

Pile A

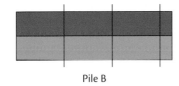

Pile B

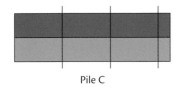

Pile C

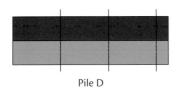

Pile D

5. Set 1 of each pile (A, B, C, and D) aside for Block B and begin piecing Block A.

Block A

All A blocks must be the same.

1. Sew an A pile square and a B pile square together as shown to make Unit 1. Be careful to keep the orientation of the squares the same each time you make Unit 1.

2. Make the following number of Unit 1's:

Crib: 6   Lap: 10   Twin: 12
Queen: 24   King: 32

There will be extra squares left over in the lap and king sizes.

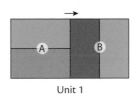

Unit 1

3. Sew a C pile square and a D pile square together as shown to make Unit 2. Be sure to keep the orientation of the squares the same each time you make Unit 2.

4. Make the following number of Unit 2's:

Crib: 6   Lap: 10   Twin: 12
Queen: 24   King: 32

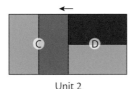

Unit 2

5. Sew a Unit 1 and a Unit 2 together as shown; the orientation of the units must be the same every time.

6. Make the following number of blocks:

Crib: 6   Lap: 10   Twin: 12
Queen: 24   King: 32

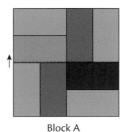

Block A

7. Set the A blocks aside. It's time to move on to the B blocks.

Block B

All B blocks must be the same.

1. Grab the 4 piles for Block B that you set aside earlier.

2. Sew a B pile square and an A pile square together as shown to make Unit 3. Be careful to keep the orientation of the squares the same each time you make Unit 3. Notice that the order is reversed from Unit 1 of Block A; the B square is now on the left.

3. Make the following number of Unit 3's:

Crib: 6   Lap: 10   Twin: 12
Queen: 24   King: 32

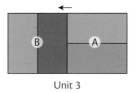

Unit 3

4. Sew a D pile square and a C pile square together as shown to make Unit 4. Keep the orientation of the squares the same each time you make Unit 4. Again, notice that the D square is now on the left.

5. Make the following number of Unit 4's:

Crib: 6   Lap: 10   Twin: 12
Queen: 24   King: 32

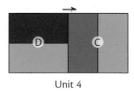

Unit 4

6. Sew a Unit 3 and a Unit 4 together as shown; the orientation of the units must be the same every time.

7. Make the following number of blocks:

Crib: 6   Lap: 10   Twin: 12   Queen: 24   King: 32

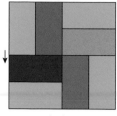

Block B

Notice the different orientation of the fabrics in the 2 blocks. The blocks should measure 12½″ × 12½″.

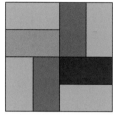 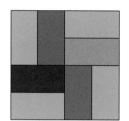

Block A   Block B

TRIMMING THE BLOCKS

See complete squaring and wonky technique instructions (pages 9–12).

1. Using the center of each block for orientation, square the blocks to measure 12″ × 12″ (page 9).

2. Place the A blocks in one pile and the B blocks in another pile. You should have 2 equal piles.

Block A

1. Place the marked square ruler at an angle on the block as shown, so that the corners of the 10½″ × 10½″ marked square touch each edge of the block and the center of the marked square (5¼″) is directly over the center seam. Trim (page 10).

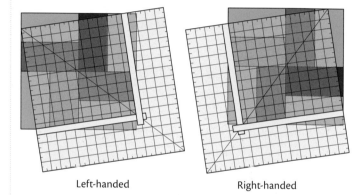

Left-handed   Right-handed

Correct ruler angle for first 2 cuts of Block A

2. Rotate the block and square the other 2 sides of the block to measure 10½″ × 10½″ (page 11).

Block A

3. Trim all the A blocks in the same way, with the angle of the ruler the same every time.

Block B

❈ note

Pay attention to the angle of the ruler—it should be different than the angle used for Block A.

1. Place the marked square ruler at an angle as shown, so that the corners of the 10½″ × 10½″ marked square touch each edge of the block and the center of the square (5¼″ mark) is directly over the center seam (page 11). Notice the difference from the angle of Block A. Trim.

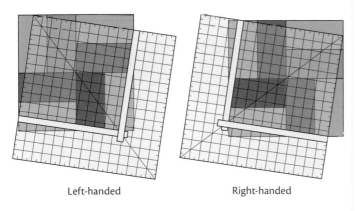

Left-handed   Right-handed

Correct ruler angle for first 2 cuts of Block B

2. Rotate the block and square the other 2 sides of the block to measure 10½″ × 10½″ (page 12).

3. Trim all the B blocks in the same way, with the angle of the ruler the same every time.

Block B

QUILT CONSTRUCTION

1. Place the blocks in rows, alternating the A and B blocks.

2. Now have some fun with them—rotate the blocks and see what happens. Go with the setting you like. I chose the one shown.

3. Sew the blocks into rows, alternating the pressing direction of the seams. Press the seams to the right in the first row, to the left in the second row, to the right in the third row, and so on.

4. Sew the rows together, matching the seams.

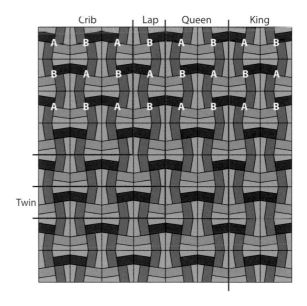

BORDERS

It's time to grab those border strips we cut earlier.

This quilt has 4 borders. Border 2 has several options; choose which option you like best from Options for Border 2 (pages 61–63).

See General Border Instructions (page 60) to measure correct border lengths. None of us sews an exact ¼″ seam. Some of us sew a generous ¼″, and yet our quilt tops are smaller than the quilt tops of those of us who sew scant ¼″ seams. For this reason it is always a good idea to measure your quilt to get the correct border strip length needed every time you add a border.

See Bodacious Border Techniques and Options (pages 60–63) for complete sewing instructions for all borders.

	CRIB	LAP	TWIN	QUEEN	KING
Border 1	2 strips 1½″ × 30½″ 2 strips 1½″ × 42½″	2 strips 2″ × 40½″ 2 strips 2″ × 62½″	2 strips 2″ × 40½″ 2 strips 2″ × 63½″	2 strips 2″ × 60½″ 2 strips 2″ × 83½″	2 strips 2″ × 80½″ 2 strips 2″ × 83½″
Border 2	2 strips 2½″ × 32½″ 2 strips 2½″ × 46½″	2 strips 3½″ × 40½″ (top and bottom only)	2 strips ½″ × 43½″ 2 strips 3½″ × 69½″	2 strips 3½″ × 63½″ 2 strips 3½″ × 89½″	2 strips 3½″ × 83½″ 2 strips 3½″ × 89½″
Border 3	2 strips 1½″ × 36½″ 2 strips 1½″ × 48½″	2 strips 2″ × 40½″ (top and bottom only)	2 strips 2″ × 49½″ 2 strips 2″ × 72½″	2 strips 2″ × 69½″ 2 strips 2″ × 92½″	2 strips 2″ × 89½″ 2 strips 2″ × 92½″
Border 4	2 strips 3½″ × 38½″ 2 strips 3½″ × 54½″	2 strips 6½″ × 43½″ 2 strips 6½″ × 74½″	2 strips 6½″ × 52½″ 2 strips 6½″ × 84½″	2 strips 8½″ × 72½″ 2 strips 8½″ × 108½″	2 strips 8½″ × 92½″ 2 strips 8½″ × 108½″

Zensational II, 44″ × 54″
Quilt made by Judy Hugo
and quilted by Nancy Frank.
Border 2 uses option 3 (page 62).

Flights of Fancy
COTTON REEL BLOCK

64" × 84"
Quilt made by Judy Hugo
and quilted by Karen Gibbs.
Border 2 uses option 3
(page 62).

■ **Finished Cotton Reel block size: 10" × 10"**

The basis for this quilt is the traditional Cotton Reel block, which is made with half-square triangles. It is another super-easy block to piece and, when wonky cut, gives a playful, almost whimsical feel.

MATERIALS

	CRIB 44″ × 54″	LAP 55″ × 74″	TWIN 64″ × 84″	QUEEN 88″ × 108″	KING 108″ × 108″
Blocks: 4 fabrics*	⅞ yard of each fabric	1¼ yards of each fabric	1¼ yards of each fabric	2⅓ yards of each fabric	3⅛ yards of each fabric
Borders 1 and 3	½ yard	½ yard	⅞ yard	1 yard	1⅛ yards
Border 2**	⅜ yard	⅜ yard	¾ yard	⅞ yard	1 yard
Border 4	⅝ yard	1¼ yards	1½ yards	2½ yards	2¾ yards
Backing	3 yards	3⅝ yards	5¼ yards	8¼ yards	10 yards
Binding	½ yard	⅝ yard	⅝ yard	⅞ yard	1 yard

*4 contrasting fabrics: 2 light/medium values and 2 dark values, or similar values but contrasting texture or print

**Yardage is given without using scraps. See complete border instructions for all sizes (pages 28 and 29).

CUTTING INSTRUCTIONS

	CRIB	LAP	TWIN	QUEEN	KING
Blocks: from each fabric*	2 strips 13¼″ × wof**; subcut 2 squares 13¼″ × 13¼″ from each strip	3 strips 13¼″ × wof**; subcut 2 squares 13¼″ × 13¼″ from each strip	3 strips 13¼″ × wof**; subcut 2 squares 13¼″ × 13¼″ from each strip	6 strips 13¼″ × wof**; subcut 2 squares 13¼″ × 13¼″ from each strip	8 strips 13¼″ × wof**; subcut 2 squares 13¼″ × 13¼″ from each strip
Borders 1 and 3	8 strips 1½″ × wof	7 strips 2″ × wof	12 strips 2″ × wof	16 strips 2″ × wof	18 strips 2″ × wof
Border 2	4 strips 2½″ × wof	3 strips 3½″ × wof	6 strips 3½″ × wof	8 strips 3½″ × wof	9 strips 3½″ × wof
Border 4	5 strips 3½″ × wof	6 strips 6½″ × wof	7 strips 6½″ × wof	10 strips 8½″ × wof	11 strips 8½″ × wof

*Keep the squares cut from each fabric in a separate pile. You will have four piles.

**wof = width of fabric

PIECING THE BLOCKS

Use ¼″ seam allowances.

1. Pair a light/medium pile with a dark pile; keep these paired. Pair the remaining light/medium pile with the remaining dark pile.

2. Align 2 squares from the first pairing—a light/medium fabric with a dark fabric—right sides together.

3. Draw a diagonal line on the wrong side of 1 square.

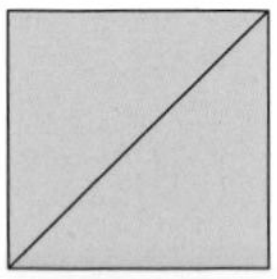

4. Sew a ¼″ seam on each side of the drawn line.

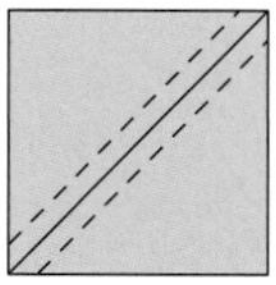

5. Cut the square in half on the drawn line to make 2 half-square triangle units. Press toward the darker fabric.

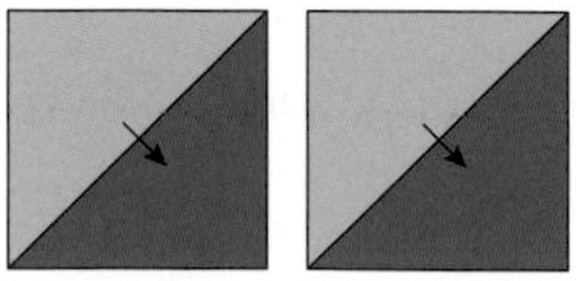

Half-square triangle units from first pairing

6. Repeat Steps 3–5 for the second pairing.

Half-square triangle units from second pairing

7. Pair a half-square triangle unit from the first pairing with a half-square triangle from the second pairing, with right sides together and hooking (nesting) the center seams. When putting the half-square triangle units together, place the light fabric on the dark fabric and the dark fabric on the light fabric.

8. Draw a diagonal line on the wrong side of 1 of the half-square triangle units.

9. Sew on each side of the drawn line using a ¼″ seam.

10. Cut on the drawn line. Press the seams in the same direction.

11. Look closely at the finished blocks and notice the slight difference in fabric placement. There are 2 types of blocks: Block A and Block B.

12. Make the following number of A blocks and the same number of B blocks:

Crib: 6   Lap: 10   Twin: 12   Queen: 24   King: 32

There will be leftover squares from the crib and lap sizes.

13. Put the A blocks in a pile and the B blocks in another pile. Each block should measure 12½″ × 12½″.

Block A   Block B

TRIMMING THE BLOCKS

See complete squaring and wonky technique instructions (pages 9–12).

1. Using the center of each block for orientation, square the blocks to measure 12″ × 12″ (page 9).

2. Keep the blocks separated into 2 piles: Block A and Block B.

Block A

> ❋ *note*
>
> *It is very important to have the ruler in the correct position every time you start the wonky cut. The correct ruler angle will be different for Block A and Block B.*

1. Place the marked square ruler at an angle on the block as shown, so that the corners of the 10½″ × 10½″ marked square touch each edge of the block and the center of the marked square (5¼″) is directly over the center seam. Trim (page 10).

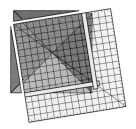

Left-handed   Right-handed

Correct ruler angle for first 2 cuts of Block A

2. Rotate the block and square the other 2 sides of the block to measure 10½″ × 10½″ (page 11).

3. Trim all the A blocks the same way, with the angle of the ruler being the same every time. Make the following number of blocks:

Crib: 6   Lap: 10   Twin: 12   Queen: 24   King: 32

Block A

Block B

❎ *note*

Pay attention to the angle of the ruler across the top of the block when you make the first wonky cut. It should be different than the angle used for Block A.

1. Place the marked square ruler at an angle, so that the corners of the 10½˝ × 10½˝ marked square touch each edge of the block and the center of the square (5¼˝ mark) is directly over the center seam (page 11). Notice the difference from the angle of Block A. Trim.

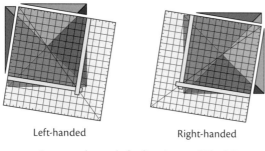

Left-handed   Right-handed

Correct ruler angle for first 2 cuts of Block B

2. Rotate the block and square the other 2 sides of the block to measure 10½˝ × 10½˝ (page 12).

3. Trim all the B blocks the same way. Make the following number of blocks:

Crib: 6   Lap: 10   Twin: 12   Queen: 24   King: 32

Block B

❎ *note*

Save all those pointy scraps that are left over after the wonky cutting. There is an option to use them in the border (page 63).

QUILT CONSTRUCTION

1. Place the blocks in rows, alternating the A and B blocks.

2. Sew the blocks into rows, alternating the pressing direction of the seams. Press the seams to the right in the first row, to the left in the second row, to the right in the third row, and so on.

3. Sew the rows together, matching the seams.

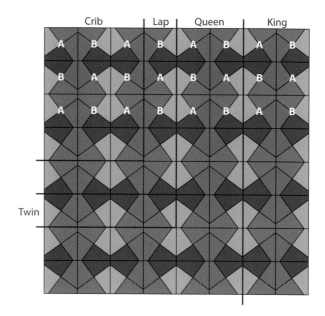

BORDERS

It's time to grab those border strips we cut earlier.

This quilt has 4 borders. Border 2 has several options; choose which option you like best from Options for Border 2 (pages 61–63).

See General Border Instructions (page 60) to measure correct border lengths. None of us sews an exact ¼˝ seam. Some of us sew a generous ¼˝, and yet our quilt tops are smaller than the quilt tops of those of us who sew scant ¼˝ seams. For this reason it is always a good idea to measure your quilt to get the correct border strip length needed every time you add a border.

See Bodacious Border Techniques and Options (pages 60–63) for complete sewing instructions for all borders.

	CRIB	LAP	TWIN	QUEEN	KING
Border 1	2 strips 1½" × 30½" 2 strips 1½" × 42½"	2 strips 2" × 40½" 2 strips 2" × 62½"	2 strips 2" × 40½" 2 strips 2" × 63½"	2 strips 2" × 60½" 2 strips 2" × 83½"	2 strips 2" × 80½" 2 strips 2" × 83½"
Border 2	2 strips 2½" × 32½" 2 strips 2½" × 46½"	2 strips 3½" × 40½" (top and bottom)	2 strips 3½" × 43½" 2 strips 3½" × 69½"	2 strips 3½" × 63½" 2 strips 3½" × 89½"	2 strips 3½" × 83½" 2 strips 3½" × 89½"
Border 3	2 strips 1½" × 36½" 2 strips 1½" × 48½"	2 strips 2" × 40½" (top and bottom)	2 strips 2" × 49½" 2 strips 2" × 72½"	2 strips 2" × 69½" 2 strips 2" × 92½"	2 strips 2" × 89½" 2 strips 2" × 92½"
Border 4	2 strips 3½" × 38½" 2 strips 3½" × 54½"	2 strips 6½" × 43½" 2 strips 6½" × 74½"	2 strips 6½" × 52½" 2 strips 6½" × 84½"	2 strips 8½" × 72½" 2 strips 8½" × 108½"	2 strips 8½" × 92½" 2 strips 8½" × 108½"

Flights of Fancy II, 64" × 84"
Quilt made by Marlous Carter
and quilted by Karen Gibbs.
Border 2 uses option 1 (page 61).

Nine-Patch Passion
NINE PATCH BLOCK

55" × 74"
Quilt made by Marlous Carter
and quilted by Karen Gibbs.
Border 2 uses option 4
(page 63).

■ **Finished Nine Patch block size: 10" × 10"**

This quilt uses the basic Nine-Patch with nine different fabrics. It is easy to piece and fun to look at. When the blocks are done, don't hesitate to play with the layout—some interesting patterns can emerge. Judy's quilt (page 35) shows an entirely different setting.

MATERIALS

	CRIB 44" × 54"	LAP 55" × 74"	TWIN 64" × 84"	QUEEN 88" × 108"	KING 108" × 108"
Blocks: 9 fabrics*	⅜ yard of each fabric	½ yard of each fabric	½ yard of each fabric	⅞ yard of each fabric	1⅛ yards of each fabric
Borders 1 and 3	½ yard	½ yard	⅞ yard	1 yard	1⅛ yards
Border 2**	⅜ yard	⅜ yard	¾ yard	⅞ yard	1 yard
Border 4	⅝ yard	1¼ yards	1½ yards	2½ yards	2¾ yards
Backing	3 yards	3⅝ yards	5¼ yards	8¼ yards	10 yards
Binding	½ yard	⅝ yard	⅝ yard	⅞ yard	1 yard

*9 contrasting fabrics: from light to dark values or similar values with distinct prints

**Yardage is given without using scraps. See complete border instructions for all sizes (pages 34 and 35).

CUTTING INSTRUCTIONS

	CRIB	LAP	TWIN	QUEEN	KING
Blocks: from each fabric*	2 strips 4½" × wof**	3 strips 4½" × wof**	3 strips 4½" × wof**	6 strips 4½" × wof**	8 strips 4½" × wof**
Borders 1 and 3	8 strips 1½" × wof	7 strips 2" × wof	12 strips 2" × wof	16 strips 2" × wof	18 strips 2" × wof
Border 2	4 strips 2½" × wof	3 strips 3½" × wof	6 strips 3½" × wof	8 strips 3½" × wof	9 strips 3½" × wof
Border 4	5 strips 3½" × wof	6 strips 6½" × wof	7 strips 6½" × wof	10 strips 8½" × wof	11 strips 8½" × wof

*Keep the strips cut from each fabric in a separate pile. You will have nine piles.

**wof = width of fabric

PIECING THE BLOCKS

Use ¼˝ seam allowances.

1. Sort the fabric strips into 3 sets of 3 different fabrics; keep the fabric groupings the same in each strip set.

2. Sew the fabric strips together in groups of 3, keeping the order the same in each set. Press following the arrows. Make the following number of strip sets from each grouping:

Crib: 2   Lap: 3   Twin: 3   Queen: 6   King: 8

Strip Set A

Strip Set B

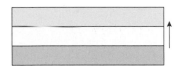

Strip Set C

3. From each strip set, cut 8 units 4½˝ × 12½˝. Keep the rectangles of each strip set in a pile. You will have 3 piles.

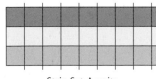

Strip Set A units

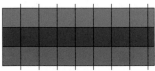

Strip Set B units

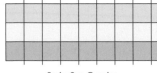

Strip Set C units

4. Sew a Strip Set A unit to a Strip Set B unit.

Sew A to B.

5. Sew a Strip Set C unit to the Strip Set B side of the A/B unit.

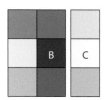

Sew C to B.

6. Make all the blocks exactly the same. Make the following number of blocks:

Crib: 12   Lap: 20   Twin: 24   Queen: 48   King: 64

Each block should measure 12½˝ × 12½˝.

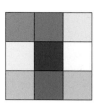

Block

TRIMMING THE BLOCKS

See pages 9–12 for complete squaring and wonky cutting instructions.

1. Divide the blocks into 2 equal piles and label them A and B.

2. Press all the seams in Block A in one direction and all the seams in Block B in the opposite direction. When it comes time to sew the blocks together for the quilt top, it will be easier to match the seams.

3. Using the center of each block for orientation, square the blocks to measure 12″ × 12″ (page 9).

Block A

> ❖ *note*
>
> *It is very important to have the ruler in the correct position every time you start the wonky cut. The correct ruler angle will be different for Block A and Block B.*

1. Place the marked square ruler at an angle on the block, so that the corners of the 10½″ × 10½″ marked square touch each edge of the block and the center of the marked square (5¼″) is directly over the center of the block. Trim (page 10).

> ✳ TIP
>
> There is no center seam in this block, so mark the center with a flower-head pin.

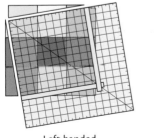

Left-handed   Right-handed

Correct ruler angle for first 2 cuts of Block A

2. Rotate the block and square the other 2 sides of the block to measure 10½″ × 10½″ (page 11).

3. Make the following number of blocks:

Crib: 6   Lap: 10   Twin: 12   Queen: 24   King: 32

Block A

4. Trim all the A blocks in the same way, with the angle of the ruler the same every time.

Block B

> ❖ *note*
>
> *Pay attention to the angle of the ruler across the top of the block when you make the first wonky cut on each block. The angle should be different than the angle used for Block A.*

1. Place the marked square ruler at an angle, so that the corners of the 10½″ × 10½″ marked square touch each edge of the block and the center of the square (5¼″ mark) is directly over the center seam (page 11). Notice the difference from the angle of Block A. Trim.

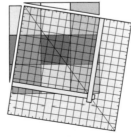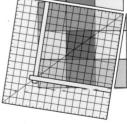

Left-handed   Right-handed

Correct ruler angle for first 2 cuts of Block B

2. Rotate the block and square the other 2 sides of the block to measure 10½″ × 10½″ (page 12).

3. Trim all the B blocks the same way. Make the following number of blocks:

Crib: 6   Lap: 10   Twin: 12   Queen: 24   King: 32

Block B

 note

Save all those pointy scraps that are left over after the wonky cutting. There is an option to use them in Border 2, should you want to. See Option 4 in Bodacious Border Techniques and Options (page 63).

QUILT CONSTRUCTION

1. Place the blocks in rows, starting each row with a B block and then alternating A and B blocks.

2. Now have some fun with them—rotate the blocks and see what happens. See *Nine-Patch Passion II* (page 35) for a different setting.

3. Sew the blocks into rows, alternating the pressing direction of the seams. Press the seams to the right in the first row, to the left in the second row, to the right in the third row, and so on.

4. Sew the rows together, matching the seams.

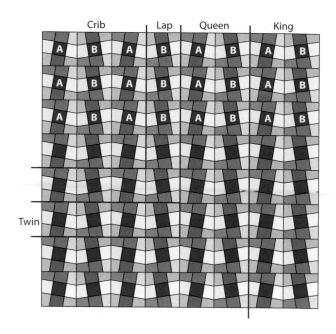

BORDERS

It's time to grab those border strips we cut earlier.

This quilt has 4 borders. Border 2 has several options; choose which option you like best from Options for Border 2 (pages 61–63).

See General Border Instructions (page 60) to measure correct border lengths. None of us sews an exact ¼″ seam. Some of us sew a generous ¼″, and yet our quilt tops are smaller than the quilt tops of those of us who sew scant ¼″ seams. For this reason it is always a good idea to measure your quilt to get the correct border strip length needed every time you add a border.

See Bodacious Border Techniques and Options (pages 60–63) for complete sewing instructions for all borders.

	CRIB	LAP	TWIN	QUEEN	KING
Border 1	2 strips 1½″ × 30½″ 2 strips 1½″ × 42½″	2 strips 2″ × 40½″ 2 strips 2″ × 62½″	2 strips 2″ × 40½″ 2 strips 2″ × 63½″	2 strips 2″ × 60½″ 2 strips 2″ × 83½″	2 strips 2″ × 80½″ 2 strips 2″ × 83½″
Border 2	2 strips 2½″ × 32½″ 2 strips 2½″ × 46½″	2 strips 3½″ × 40½″ (top and bottom)	2 strips 3½″ × 43½″ 2 strips 3½″ × 69½″	2 strips 3½″ × 63½″ 2 strips 3½″ × 89½″	2 strips 3½″ × 83½″ 2 strips 3½″ × 89½″
Border 3	2 strips 1½″ × 36½″ 2 strips 1½″ × 48½″	2 strips 2″ × 40½″ (top and bottom)	2 strips 2″ × 49½″ 2 strips 2″ × 72½″	2 strips 2″ × 69½″ 2 strips 2″ × 92½″	2 strips 2″ × 89½″ 2 strips 2″ × 92½″
Border 4	2 strips 3½″ × 38½″ 2 strips 3½″ × 54½″	2 strips 6½″ × 43½″ 2 strips 6½″ × 74½″	2 strips 6½″ × 52½″ 2 strips 6½″ × 84½″	2 strips 8½″ × 72½″ 2 strips 8½″ × 108½″	2 strips 8½″ × 92½″ 2 strips 8½″ × 108½″

Nine-Patch Passion II, 64″ × 84″
Quilt made by Judy Hugo
and quilted by Nancy Frank.
The blocks are laid out alternating the A and B blocks.
Border 2 uses options 3 and 4 (pages 62 and 63).

Bejeweled
DOUBLE SQUARE BLOCK

64″ × 84″
Quilt made by Marlous Carter and quilted by Karen Gibbs. Border 2 uses options 1 and 2 (pages 61 and 62).

■ **Finished Double Square block size: 10″ × 10″**

Here, the Double Square block, which is made with four half-square triangles, is wonky cut to create a secondary pattern of diamonds. As with all the quilts in this book, this one is easy to piece and easy to wonky cut.

MATERIALS

	CRIB 44″ × 54″	LAP 55″ × 74″	TWIN 64″ × 84″	QUEEN 88″ × 108″	KING 108″ × 108″
Blocks: 8 fabrics*	½ yard of each fabric	½ yard of each fabric	⅔ yard of each fabric	1⅛ yards of each fabric	1½ yards of each fabric
Borders 1 and 3	½ yard	½ yard	⅞ yard	1 yard	1⅛ yards
Border 2**	⅜ yard	⅜ yard	¾ yard	⅞ yard	1 yard
Border 4	⅝ yard	1¼ yards	1½ yards	2½ yards	2¾ yards
Backing	3 yards	3⅝ yards	5¼ yards	8¼ yards	10 yards
Binding	½ yard	⅝ yard	⅝ yard	⅞ yard	1 yard

*8 different fabrics: 4 light/medium and 4 dark fabrics

**Yardage is given without using scraps. See complete border instructions for all sizes (pages 40 and 41).

CUTTING INSTRUCTIONS

	CRIB	LAP	TWIN	QUEEN	KING
Blocks: from each fabric*	2 strips 7″ × wof**; subcut 5 squares 7″ × 7″ from each strip	2 strips 7″ × wof**; subcut 5 squares 7″ × 7″ from each strip.	3 strips 7″ × wof**; subcut 5 squares 7″ × 7″ from each strip	5 strips 7″ × wof**; subcut 5 squares 7″ × 7″ from each strip	7 strips 7″ × wof**; subcut 5 squares 7″ × 7″ from each strip
Borders 1 and 3	8 strips 1½″ × wof	7 strips 2″ × wof	12 strips 2″ × wof	16 strips 2″ × wof	18 strips 2″ × wof
Border 2	4 strips 2½″ × wof	3 strips 3½″ × wof	6 strips 3½″ × wof	8 strips 3½″ × wof	9 strips 3½″ × wof
Border 4	5 strips 3½″ × wof	6 strips 6½″ × wof	7 strips 6½″ × wof	10 strips 8½″ × wof	12 strips 8½″ × wof

*Keep the squares cut from each fabric in a separate pile. You will have eight piles.

**wof = width of fabric

PIECING THE BLOCKS

Use ¼″ seam allowances.

Block A

1. Draw a diagonal line on the wrong side of each of the light/medium squares.

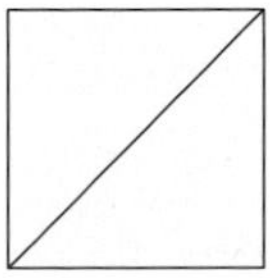

2. Pair a light/medium square with a dark square, keeping the pairing the same for all the blocks. You will have 4 different pair groupings.

3. With right sides together, sew on each side of the drawn line with a ¼″ seam.

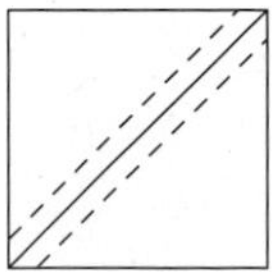

4. Cut on the drawn line and press toward the dark fabric. From each fabric pair you will get 2 half-square triangle units.

Fabric pair A

Fabric pair B

Fabric pair C

Fabric pair D

5. Separate the 2 matching half-square triangle units into 2 piles (keeping each pairing together). You will have 8 piles. You will need the following number of fabric pair half-square triangle units in each pile:

Crib: 6   Lap: 10   Twin: 12
Queen: 24   King: 32

There will be extra units for all sizes except the lap size.

6. Take a pile of each fabric pair for Block A and set the rest of the half-square triangle unit piles aside for Block B.

7. Look carefully at the half-square fabric pair placement in the block; the placement must stay the same for every Block A you make.

8. Sew an A half-square triangle unit and a B half-square triangle unit together.

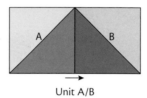

Unit A/B

9. Sew a C half-square triangle and a D half-square triangle together as shown.

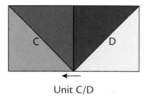

Unit C/D

10. Sew the units from Steps 8 and 9 together to complete Block A.

11. Make the following number of blocks:

Crib: 6   Lap: 10   Twin: 12
Queen: 24   King: 32

Make all the A blocks exactly the same. The blocks should measure 12¾″ × 12¾″.

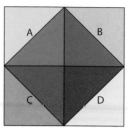

Block A

Block B

1. Look carefully at the half-square triangle placement in the block; the placement must stay the same for each Block B.

2. Sew a B half-square triangle unit and an A half-square triangle unit together. Note that the positioning is switched from that of Block A. The B half-square triangle is on the right and the A half-square triangle is on the left.

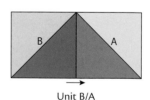

Unit B/A

3. Sew a D half-square triangle unit and a C half-square triangle unit together (again, the positioning is switched from Block A).

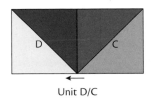

Unit D/C

4. Sew these units together to complete Block B.

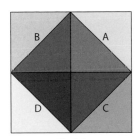

Block B

5. Make all the B blocks exactly the same. Make the following number of blocks:

Crib: 6   Lap: 10   Twin: 12   Queen: 24   King: 32

The blocks should measure 12¾″ × 12¾″.

Now it's on to the wonky technique. Ready?

TRIMMING THE BLOCKS

See complete squaring and wonky technique instructions (pages 9–12).

Do not mix the A and B blocks when squaring.

1. Using the center of each block for orientation, square the blocks to measure 12″ × 12″ (page 9).

2. Look at the blocks in each pile and double-check that all the A blocks are in one pile and all the B blocks are in the other.

⊞ *note*

It is very important to have the ruler in the correct position every time you start the wonky cut. The correct ruler angle will be different for Block A and Block B.

Block A

1. Place the marked square ruler at an angle on the block, so that the corners of the 10½″ × 10½″ marked square touch each edge of the block and the center of the marked square (5¼″) is directly over the center seam. Trim (page 10).

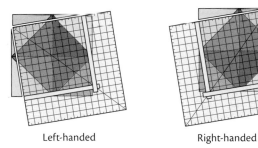

Left-handed   Right-handed

Correct ruler angle for first 2 cuts of Block A

2. Rotate the block and square the other 2 sides of the block to measure 10½″ × 10½″ (page 11). Make the following number of blocks:

Crib: 6   Lap: 10   Twin: 12   Queen: 24   King: 32

Block A

3. Trim all the A blocks in the same way, with the angle of the ruler the same every time.

Block B

⊞ *note*

Block B must always have the same ruler angle across the top of the block when you begin the wonky technique. The angle for Block B is different from the angle for Block A.

1. Place the marked square ruler at an angle on the block, so that the corners of the 10½˝ × 10½˝ marked square touch each edge of the block and the center of the marked square (5¼˝) is directly over the center seam. Trim (page 11).

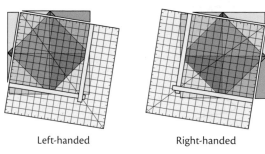

Left-handed   Right-handed

Correct ruler angle for first 2 cuts of Block B

2. Rotate the block and square the other 2 sides of the block to measure 10½˝ × 10½˝ (page 12). Make the following number of blocks:

Crib: 6   Lap: 10   Twin: 12   Queen: 24   King: 32

Block B

3. Trim all the B blocks the same way.

⊞ *note*

Save all those pointy scraps that are left over after the wonky cutting. There is an option to use them in the border (page 63), and you want to keep all your options open, right?

QUILT CONSTRUCTION

1. Place the blocks in rows, alternating the A and B blocks.

2. Sew the blocks into rows, alternating the pressing direction of the seams. Press the seams to the right in the first row, to the left in the second row, to the right in the third row, and so on.

3. Sew the rows together, matching the seams.

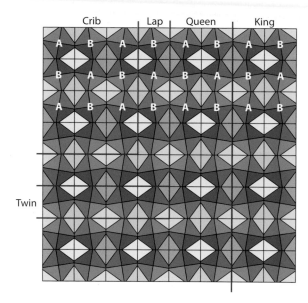

BORDERS

It's time to grab those border strips we cut earlier.

This quilt has 4 borders. Border 2 has several options; choose which option you like best from Options for Border 2 (pages 61–63).

See General Border Instructions (page 60) to measure correct border lengths. None of us sews an exact ¼˝ seam. Some of us sew a generous ¼˝, and yet our quilt tops are smaller than the quilt tops of those of us who sew scant ¼˝ seams. For this reason it is always a good idea to measure your quilt to get the correct border strip length needed every time you add a border.

See Bodacious Border Techniques and Options (pages 60–63) for complete sewing instructions for all borders.

	CRIB	LAP	TWIN	QUEEN	KING
Border 1	2 strips 1½″ × 30½″ 2 strips 1½″ × 42½″	2 strips 2″ × 40½″ 2 strips 2″ × 62½″	2 strips 2″ × 40½″ 2 strips 2″ × 63½″	2 strips 2″ × 60½″ 2 strips 2″ × 83½″	2 strips 2″ × 80½″ 2 strips 2″ × 83½″
Border 2	2 strips 2½″ × 32½″ 2 strips 2½″ × 46½″	2 strips 3½″ × 40½″ (top and bottom only)	2 strips 3½″ × 43½″ 2 strips 3½″ × 69½″	2 strips 3½″ × 63½″ 2 strips 3½″ × 89½″	2 strips 3½″ × 83½″ 2 strips 3½″ × 89½″
Border 3	2 strips 1½″ × 36½″ 2 strips 1½″ × 48½″	2 strips 2″ × 40½″ (top and bottom only)	2 strips 2″ × 49½″ 2 strips 2″ × 72½″	2 strips 2″ × 69½″ 2 strips 2″ × 92½″	2 strips 2″ × 89½″ 2 strips 2″ × 92½″
Border 4	2 strips 3½″ × 38½″ 2 strips 3½″ × 54½″	2 strips 6½″ × 43½″ 2 strips 6½″ × 74½″	2 strips 6½″ × 52½″ 2 strips 6½″ × 84½″	2 strips 8½″ × 72½″ 2 strips 8½″ × 108½″	2 strips 8½″ × 92½″ 2 strips 8½″ × 108½″

Bejeweled II, 55″ × 74″
Quilt made by Judy Hugo
and quilted by Nancy Frank.
Border 2 uses option 1 (page 61).

Squared Away
COURTHOUSE STEPS BLOCK

64" × 84"
Quilt made by Marlous Carter
and quilted by Karen Gibbs.
Border 2 uses options 1, 3, and 4
(pages 61–63).

■ **Finished Courthouse Steps block size:** 10" × 10"

The fabulously easy Courthouse Steps pattern is given a small face-lift by adding the wonky cut and some simple rough-edge appliqué. You just can't go wrong with this quilt!

MATERIALS

	CRIB 44" × 54"	LAP 55" × 74"	TWIN 64" × 84"	QUEEN 88" × 108"	KING 108" × 108"
Blocks*	6 fat quarters ⅓ yard contrast	10 fat quarters ½ yard contrast	12 fat quarters ½ yard contrast	24 fat quarters ⅞ yard contrast	32 fat quarters 1⅛ yards contrast
Borders 1 and 3	½ yard	½ yard	⅞ yard	1 yard	1⅛ yards
Border 2**	⅜ yard	⅜ yard	¾ yard	⅞ yard	1 yard
Border 4	⅝ yard	1¼ yards	1½ yards	2½ yards	2¾ yards
Backing	3 yards	3⅝ yards	5¼ yards	8¼ yards	10 yards
Binding	½ yard	⅝ yard	⅝ yard	⅞ yard	1 yard

*The contrast fabric is for the centers of all the blocks.

**Yardage is given without using scraps. See complete border instructions for all sizes (pages 46 and 47).

CUTTING INSTRUCTIONS

	CRIB	LAP	TWIN	QUEEN	KING
From each fat quarter*	7 strips 2½" × 22"	7 strips 2½" × 22"	7 strips 2½" × 22"	7 strips 2½" × 22"	7 strips 2½" × 22"
	*Using 4 strips**, from each strip cut:*				
	1 strip 2½" × 12½" 1 strip 2½" × 8½"	1 strip 2½" × 12½" 1 strip 2½" × 8½"	1 strip 2½" × 12½" 1 strip 2½" × 8½"	1 strip 2½" × 12½" 1 strip 2½" × 8½"	1 strip 2½" × 12½" 1 strip 2½" × 8½"
	Using 2 strips, from each strip cut:				
	2 strips 2½" × 8½" 1 square 2" × 2"	2 strips 2½" × 8½" 1 square 2" × 2"	2 strips 2½" × 8½" 1 square 2" × 2"	2 strips 2½" × 8½" 1 square 2" × 2"	2 strips 2½" × 8½" 1 square 2" × 2"
	Using 1 strip, cut:				
	4 strips 2½" × 4½"	4 strips 2½" × 4½"	4 strips 2½" × 4½"	4 strips 2½" × 4½"	4 strips 2½" × 4½"
Contrast fabric	2 strips 4½" × wof***	3 strips 4½" × wof***	3 strips 4½" × wof***	6 strips 4½" × wof***	8 strips 4½" × wof***
	From each strip cut:				
	9 squares 4½" × 4½"	9 squares 4½" × 4½"	9 squares 4½" × 4½"	9 squares 4½" × 4½"	9 squares 4½" × 4½"
Borders 1 and 3	8 strips 1½" × wof	7 strips 2" × wof	12 strips 2" × wof	16 strips 2" × wof	18 strips 2" × wof
Border 2	4 strips 2½" × wof	3 strips 3½" × wof	6 strips 3½" × wof	8 strips 3½" × wof	9 strips 3½" × wof
Border 4	5 strips 3½" × wof	6 strips 6½" × wof	7 strips 6½" × wof	10 strips 8½" × wof	12 strips 8½" × wof

*Keep the strips cut from each of the fat quarters together.

**When subcutting the strips, work with only the seven strips cut from one fat quarter at a time.

***wof = width of fabric

PIECING THE BLOCKS

Use ¼″ seam allowances.

Sorting the Strips

1. Sort the cut strips into the following groups, but don't mix fabrics. There will be a pile A and a pile B *for each fabric.*

Pile A: 2 strips 2½″ × 8½″ and 2 strips 2½″ × 4½″

Pile B: 2 strips 2½″ × 12½″ and 2 strips 2½″ × 8½″

2. Put all the 2″ × 2″ squares in a separate pile to use later. These will be raw-edge appliquéd onto the centers later.

3. Each block is made using 1 center 4½″ × 4½″ square and 1 group from pile A and 1 group from pile B (different fabrics).

Constructing the Blocks

All the blocks are made in exactly the same way.

1. Gather a 4½″ × 4½″ center square and 1 pile A.

2. Sew a 2½″ × 4½″ rectangle to the top of the center square. Sew the other 2½″ × 4½″ rectangle to the bottom. Press both seams to the outside.

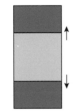

Sew rectangles to square.

3. Sew a 2½″ × 8½″ rectangle to each side of the block and press to the outside.

Sew rectangles to block.

4. Grab a pile B that is *not* the same fabric as you just used.

5. Sew 2½″ × 8½″ rectangles to the top and bottom of the block. Press to the outside.

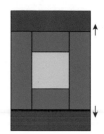

Sew rectangles to block.

6. Sew 2½″ × 12½″ rectangles to each side of the block and press to the outside.

7. Make the following number of blocks:

Crib: 12   Lap: 20   Twin: 24   Queen: 48   King: 64

Make all the blocks in exactly the same way, being sure to use 2 different fabric piles to surround the center contrast square in each block. The blocks should measure 12½″ × 12½″.

Block

TRIMMING THE BLOCKS

See complete squaring and wonky technique instructions (pages 9–12).

1. Using the center of each block for orientation, square all the blocks to measure 12″ × 12″ (page 9).

2. Separate the blocks into 2 equal piles and label them A and B.

 note

Look closely at the angle of your ruler when you begin the wonky cut. The angle of the ruler will be different for A and B blocks.

Block A

1. Place the marked square ruler at an angle on the block as shown, so that the corners of the 10½″ × 10½″ marked square touch each edge of the block and the center of the marked square (5¼″) is directly over the center of the block. Trim (page 10).

* TIP

Use a flower head pin to mark the center of the block.

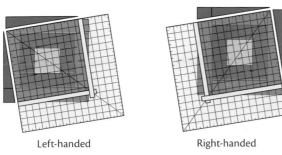

Left-handed   Right-handed

Correct ruler angle for first 2 cuts of Block A

2. Rotate the block and square the other 2 sides of the block to measure 10½″ × 10½″ (page 11).

3. Make the following number of A blocks.

Crib: 6   Lap: 10   Twin: 12   Queen: 24   King: 32

Block A

* TIP

Always save those pointy scraps left over after the wonky cutting. These can be used in one of the border options (page 63), and we should always keep all our options open.

Block B

⊞ *note*

The B blocks are trimmed in exactly the same way, but the ruler is at a different angle.

1. Place the marked square ruler at an angle, so that the corners of the 10½″ × 10½″ marked square touch each edge of the block and the center of the square (5¼″ mark) is directly over the center seam (page 11). Notice the difference from the angle of Block A. Trim.

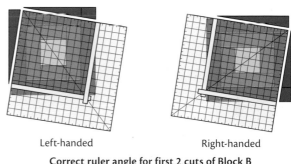

Left-handed   Right-handed

Correct ruler angle for first 2 cuts of Block B

2. Rotate the block and square the other 2 sides of the block to measure 10½″ × 10½″ (page 12).

3. Make the following number of B blocks:

Crib: 6   Lap: 10   Twin: 12   Queen: 24   King: 32

Block B

RAW-EDGE APPLIQUÉ CENTER SQUARES

> ⊞ *note*
>
> *Raw-edge appliqué is a super-easy technique that adds an extra spark to any quilt.*

Remember all those 2″ × 2″ squares you cut and set aside? Well, now's the time to gather them.

Do not mix the A pile and B pile blocks. Work through a single pile at a time.

1. Beginning with an A pile block, choose a 2″ × 2″ square that is different from the 2 fabrics used in the block already.

2. On the wrong side of the 2″ × 2″ square, dab a little glue along the edges of the fabric.

3. Place the square right side up in the center of the block and line up the edges with the wonky *cut* edges of the block, so that visually the appliquéd block is not angled. Press down with your hand to secure.

4. With a regular straight stitch, stitch along the edge of the appliqué square (about ⅛″ in) to secure.

5. Appliqué a center square to every A and B block, being sure that the fabric is different from the fabrics already used in the block.

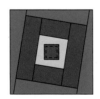
Block A

Block B

> ⊞ *note*
>
> *When quilting this quilt, stitch over the rough-edge appliquéd pieces.*

QUILT CONSTRUCTION

1. Place the blocks in rows, alternating the A and B blocks.

2. Sew the blocks into rows, alternating the pressing direction of the seams. Press the seams to the right in the first row, to the left in the second row, to the right in the third row, and so on.

3. Sew the rows together, matching the seams.

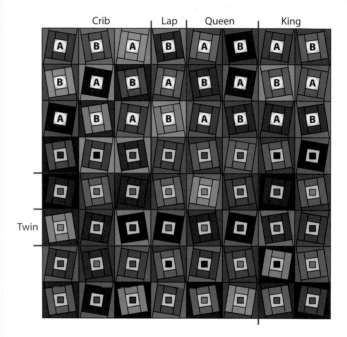

BORDERS

It's time to grab those border strips we cut earlier.

This quilt has 4 borders. Border 2 has several options; choose which option you like best from Options for Border 2 (pages 61–63).

See General Border Instructions (page 60) to measure correct border lengths. None of us sews an exact ¼″ seam. Some of us sew a generous ¼″, and yet our quilt tops are smaller than the quilt tops of those of us who sew scant ¼″ seams. For this reason it is always a good idea to measure your quilt to get the correct border strip length needed every time you add a border.

See Bodacious Border Techniques and Options (pages 60–63) for complete sewing instructions for all borders.

	CRIB	LAP	TWIN	QUEEN	KING
Border 1	2 strips 1½" × 30½" 2 strips 1½" × 42½"	2 strips 2" × 40½" 2 strips 2" × 62½"	2 strips 2" × 40½" 2 strips 2" × 63½"	2 strips 2" × 60½" 2 strips 2" × 83½"	2 strips 2" × 80½" 2 strips 2" × 83½"
Border 2	2 strips 2½" × 32½" 2 strips 2½" × 46½"	2 strips 3½" × 40½" (top and bottom only)	2 strips 3½" × 43½" 2 strips 3½" × 69½"	2 strips 3½" × 63½" 2 strips 3½" × 89½"	2 strips 3½" × 83½" 2 strips 3½" × 89½"
Border 3	2 strips 1½" × 36½" 2 strips 1½" × 48½"	2 strips 2" × 40½" (top and bottom only)	2 strips 2" × 49½" 2 strips 2" × 72½"	2 strips 2" × 69½" 2 strips 2" × 92½"	2 strips 2" × 89½" 2 strips 2" × 92½"
Border 4	2 strips 3½" × 38½" 2 strips 3½" × 54½"	2 strips 6½" × 43½" 2 strips 6½" × 74½"	2 strips 6½" × 52½" 2 strips 6½" × 84½"	2 strips 8½" × 72½" 2 strips 8½" × 108½"	2 strips 8½" × 92½" 2 strips 8½" × 108½"

Squared Away II, 55" × 74"
Quilt made by Judy Hugo
and quilted by Nancy Frank.
Border 2 uses options 1 and 2 (pages 61 and 62).

Whimsy
COTTON REEL BLOCK

69″ × 84½″
Quilt made by Marlous Carter
and quilted by Karen Gibbs.
Border 2 uses option 3
(page 62).

■ **Finished Cotton Reel block size:** 14″ × 14″

*This quilt has a scrappy, almost carefree feel because
of the number of fat quarters used.*

MATERIALS

	LAP 44½" × 69"	TWIN 69" × 84½"	QUEEN 88½" × 104"
Blocks and Border 2*	12 fat quarters: 6 medium and 6 dark	24 fat quarters: 12 medium and 12 dark	40 fat quarters: 20 medium and 20 dark
Sashing, Border 1, and Border 3	⅝ yard	1⅛ yards	1¾ yards
Border 4	1¼ yards	1⅝ yards	2¼ yards
Backing	3⅛ yards	5⅜ yards	8¼ yards
Binding	½ yard	⅝ yard	⅞ yard

*Yardage is given without using scraps. See complete border instructions for all sizes (pages 53 and 54).

CUTTING INSTRUCTIONS

	LAP	TWIN	QUEEN
Blocks: from each fat quarter	1 strip 3½" × 21"* 1 strip 2½" × 21"** 1 strip 10¼" × 21" Subcut 2 squares 10¼" × 10¼" from each 10¼" strip.***	1 strip 3½" × 21"* 1 strip 2½" × 21"** 1 strip 10¼" × 21" Subcut 2 squares 10¼" × 10¼" from each 10¼" strip.***	1 strip 3½" × 21"* 1 strip 2½" × 21"** 1 strip 10¼" × 21" Subcut 2 squares 10¼" × 10¼" from each 10¼" strip.***
Sashing, Border 1 (outer sashing strip), and Border 3	9 strips 2" × wof****	19 strips 2" × wof****	28 strips 2" × wof****
Border 4	6 strips 6½" × wof	8 strips 6½" × wof	9 strips 8½" × wof

*Set aside to use in Border 2. Along with these strips you can use the scraps created by the wonky cut.

**Set aside to use as part of the binding (if you choose). Yardage given is without the use of these strips.

***Do not mix the 10¼" × 10¼" squares cut from each fabric.

****wof = width of fabric

BLOCK CONSTRUCTION

1. Sort the squares into groups of 4: 2 mediums and 2 darks. All 4 fabrics in the group must be different. You will have the following number of groups with 4 different fabric squares:

Lap: 6   Twin: 12   Queen: 20

2. Draw a diagonal line on the wrong side of each of the 2 medium squares in each group.

3. Take one of the groups of 4 different fabrics. Work with this group of fabrics all the way through the wonky cut process before moving on to the next group.

4. Place the squares right sides together in pairs. Each pair will have 1 square with a drawn line.

5. Using a ¼˝ seam, sew on each side of the drawn line. Do this with both pairs in the group.

Sew.

6. Cut on the line and press to the darker fabric. You will get 2 half-square triangle units from each pair.

Cut and press.

7. Take a half-square triangle unit of each fabric pair and put the 2 units right sides together. The darker fabric should lie on the lighter fabric and the center seams should nest snugly together.

8. Draw a diagonal line on the wrong side of 1 of the half-square triangles in the pair.

9. Sew with a ¼˝ seam on either side of the drawn line.

Draw line and sew.

10. Cut on the drawn line to make 2 blocks from each pairing. Each of the 4 blocks should measure approximately 9½˝ × 9½˝.

> ### ✤ *note*
>
> *Look closely at the 4 squares. There are 2 that have fabric oriented for Block A and 2 that have fabric oriented for Block B. Keep the 2 A blocks together and the 2 B blocks together; eventually these 4 blocks will be used to make 1 finished block.*

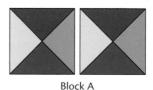

Block A

Block B

TRIMMING THE BLOCKS

See pages 9–12 for complete squaring and wonky cutting instructions.

1. Using the center of each block for orientation, square the blocks to measure 9″ × 9″ (page 9).

2. Keep the blocks divided into 2 equal piles: A blocks and B blocks.

Block A

It is very important to keep the ruler at the same angle each time you begin the wonky cut. The angle for Block A will be different than the angle for Block B.

1. Place the marked square ruler at an angle on the block, so that the corners of the 7½″ × 7½″ marked square touch each edge of the block and the center of the marked square (3¾″) is directly over the center seam. Trim (page 10).

Left-handed   Right-handed

Correct ruler angle for first 2 cuts of Block A

2. Rotate the block and square the other 2 sides of the block to measure 7½″ × 7½″ (page 11).

A blocks

3. Trim both A blocks the same way.

Block B

Pay attention to the angle of the ruler across the top of the block for the first wonky cut of each B block. It is different from Block A.

1. Place the marked square ruler at an angle, so that the corners of the 7½″ × 7½″ marked square touch each edge of the block and the center of the marked square (3¾″ mark) is directly over the center seam (page 11). Notice the difference from the angle of Block A. Trim.

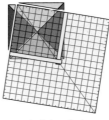
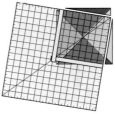

Left-handed   Right-handed

Correct ruler angle for first 2 cuts of Block B

2. Rotate the block and square the other 2 sides of the block to measure 7½″ × 7½″ (page 12).

3. Trim both B blocks the same way.

B blocks

FINISHING THE BLOCKS

Now it's time to put the 2 A blocks and the 2 B blocks together to make the finished block.

1. Sew a Block B and a Block A together, matching fabrics.

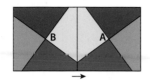

Sew A to B.

2. Sew a Block A and a Block B together, matching fabrics.

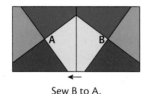

Sew B to A.

3. Sew the 2 units together, matching the fabrics, to finish the block. The block should measure 14½″ × 14½″.

Group 1 block

4. Repeat the steps from Block Construction, Step 3, through Finishing the Blocks, Step 3, for each group of 4 squares. You should have the following number of blocks:

Lap: 6   Twin: 12   Queen: 20.

QUILT CONSTRUCTION

Sashing

It's time to sew sashing to the blocks and to construct the quilt top.

1. Remember the 2″ × width of fabric (wof) strips you cut earlier? It's time to bring them back to the table.

2. You need the following total number of 2″ × wof strips for the sashing:

Lap: 7   Twin: 12   Queen: 20

3. From a strip cut 2 rectangles 2″ × 14½″. You need the following number of 2″ × 14½″ rectangles for the vertical sashing strips:

Lap: 3   Twin: 8   Queen: 15

4. Save the leftover fabric and remaining 2″ × wof strips to use later for piecing longer strips of sashing.

5. Sew a 2″ × 14½″ sashing strip to the side of a block.

Attach strip.

6. Sew a block to the other side of the sashing strip, then another sashing strip, then another block, and so on until you have sewn on the number of blocks needed for a row in the size of quilt you are making (Lap: 2 blocks across; Twin: 3 blocks across; Queen: 4 blocks across). Repeat until you have the number of rows you need (Lap: 3 rows; Twin: 4 rows; Queen: 5 rows).

Sew blocks and sashing.

7. Press the seams to the right in the first row, to the left in the second row, to the right in the third row, and so on.

8. Measure the rows, and cut and piece sashing strips as needed to obtain the right length.

9. Sew the rows together with the long horizontal sashing strips. Measure the row to double-check the length. The lengths should be approximately as follows:

Lap: 30˝ Twin: 45½˝ Queen: 61˝

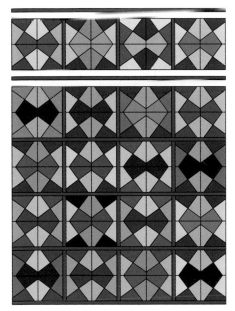

Add horizontal sashing.

 note

The outside sashing is also Border 1. Before sewing on the outside sashing strips, see the complete border instructions (at right).

10. Measure the quilt top and cut and piece the 2 vertical sashing/Border 1 strips. Attach them to the quilt top for the twin and queen sizes. For a lap-size quilt, sew Borders 1, 2, and 3 to the top and bottom before adding the outside vertical sashing.

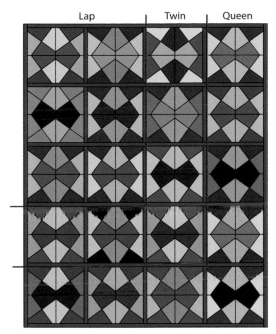

Add long vertical sashing/border strips.

BORDERS

It's time to grab those border strips we cut earlier.

This quilt has 4 borders. Border 2 has several options; choose which option you like best from Options for Border 2 (pages 61–63).

See General Border Instructions (page 60) to measure correct border lengths. None of us sews an exact ¼˝ seam. Some of us sew a generous ¼˝, and yet our quilt tops are smaller than the quilt tops of those of us who sew scant ¼˝ seams. For this reason it is always a good idea to measure your quilt to get the correct border strip length needed every time you add a border.

note

Sew Border 2 to the top and bottom first, then to the sides, using the 3½˝ × 21˝ strips cut from the fat quarters. Cut and piece as desired to make the length needed.

See Bodacious Border Techniques and Options (pages 60–63) for complete sewing instructions for all borders.

	LAP*	TWIN	QUEEN
Border 1	Sashing strip	Sashing strip	Sashing strip
Border 2	3½″ × 21″ strips cut from fat quarters: piece as needed to fit (top and bottom only)	3½″ × 21″ strips cut from fat quarters: piece as needed to fit	3½″ × 21″ strips cut from fat quarters: piece as needed to fit
Border 3	2 strips 2″ × 30″ (top and bottom only)	2 strips 2″ × 54½″ 2 strips 2″ × 73″	2 strips 2″ × 70″ 2 strips 2″ × 88½″
Border 4	2 strips 6½″ × 33″ 2 strips 6½″ × 69½″	2 strips 6½″ × 57½″ 2 strips 6½″ × 85″	2 strips 8½″ × 73″ 2 strips 8½″ × 104½″

*Sew Border 1 (top and bottom sashing strips), Border 2, and Border 3 to the top and bottom first before sewing on the side sashing strips.

Whimsy II, 53½″ × 69″
Quilt made by Judy Hugo
and quilted by Nancy Frank.
Border 2 uses option 3 (page 62).

Boardwalk
STRIP BUNDLE QUILT

55" × 74"
Quilt made by Marlous Carter
and quilted by Karen Gibbs.
Border 2 uses option 3
(page 62).

■ **Finished strip-pieced block size:** 10" × 10"

This wonderfully easy quilt uses those popular 2½"-wide strip bundles, such as Jelly Rolls or Bali Pops. So, grab a pack—or two or three—and settle down for some fun, fast, and rewarding piecing! One strip bundle usually contains 40 strips 2½" wide.

MATERIALS

	CRIB 44″ × 54″	LAP 55″ × 74″	TWIN 64″ × 84″	QUEEN 88″ × 108″	KING 108″ × 108″
Blocks	26 strips 2½″ × wof* (1 strip bundle)	44 strips 2½″ × wof* (2 strip bundles)	52 strips 2½″ × wof* (2 strip bundles)	104 strips 2½″ × wof* (3 strip bundles)	139 strips 2½″ × wof* (4 strip bundles)
Borders 1 and 3	½ yard	½ yard	⅞ yard	1 yard	1⅛ yards
Border 2**	⅜ yard	⅜ yard	¾ yard	⅞ yard	1 yard
Border 4	⅝ yard	1¼ yards	1½ yards	2½ yards	2¾ yards
Backing	3 yards	3⅝ yards	5¼ yards	8¼ yards	10 yards
Binding	½ yard	⅝ yard	⅝ yard	⅞ yard	1 yard

*wof = width of fabric

**Yardage is given without using scraps. See complete border instructions for all sizes (pages 58–59).

CUTTING INSTRUCTIONS

	CRIB	LAP	TWIN	QUEEN	KING
Blocks: from each strip, cut 4 rectangles 2½″ × 8½″*	Use 18 strips	Use 30 strips	Use 36 strips	Use 72 strips	Use 96 strips
Blocks: from each strip, cut 3 rectangles 2½″ × 12½″*	Use 8 strips	Use 14 strips	Use 16 strips	Use 32 strips	Use 43 strips
Borders 1 and 3	8 strips 1½″ × wof**	7 strips 2″ × wof**	12 strips 2″ × wof**	16 strips 2″ × wof**	18 strips 2″ × wof**
Border 2	4 strips 2½″ × wof	3 strips 3½″ × wof	6 strips 3½″ × wof	8 strips 3½″ × wof	9 strips 3½″ × wof
Border 4	5 strips 3½″ × wof	6 strips 6½″ × wof	7 strips 6½″ × wof	10 strips 8½″ × wof	12 strips 8½″ × wof

*Keep the rectangles cut from each strip together.

**wof = width of fabric

PIECING THE BLOCKS

Use ¼" seam allowances.

> ✳ TIP
>
> When I piece my blocks, I move the needle position over
> to the right one setting so I sew using a scant ¼" seam.
> This compensates for the space the thread uses when the
> seams are pressed.

1. Sort the 2½" × 8½" rectangles into groups of 6. Be sure
there are no repeats of fabric in any group.

2. Sew each group together to make an 8½" × 12½" rectangle. Press the seams in one direction.

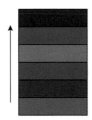

Sew rectangles.

3. Make the following number of 8½" × 12½" rectangles:

Crib: 12   Lap: 20   Twin: 24   Queen: 48   King: 64

4. Sew a 2½" × 12½" rectangle to each side of the pieced
rectangle. Press the seams to the outside.

Add rectangles to sides.

Now it's time to give the blocks some attitude. Are you
ready to wonk?

TRIMMING THE BLOCKS

*See complete squaring and wonky technique instructions
(pages 9–12).*

1. Using the center of each block for orientation, square
the blocks to measure 12" × 12" (page 9).

2. Divide the blocks into 2 equal piles and label them A
and B.

Block A

> ❖ *note*
>
> *Every time you begin the wonky cut, the center strips of
> the block need to be horizontal if cutting right-handed
> and vertical if left-handed.*

1. Place the marked square ruler at an angle on the block,
so that the corners of the 10½" × 10½" marked square touch
each edge of the block and the center of the marked square
(5¼") is directly over the center seam. Trim (page 10).

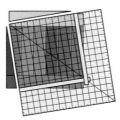 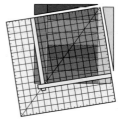

Left-handed   Right-handed

Correct ruler angle for first 2 cuts of Block A

2. Rotate the block and square the other 2 sides of the
block to measure 10½" × 10½" (page 11).

3. Trim all the A blocks in the same way, with the center
strips horizontal and the angle of the ruler the same every
time. Make the following number of blocks:

Crib: 6   Lap: 10   Twin: 12   Queen: 24   King: 32

Block A

Save the pointy scraps from trimming the blocks; these can be used in one of the options given for Border 2 (pages 61–63).

Block B

>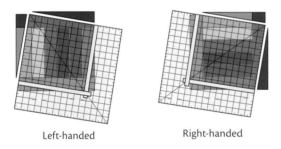
>
> **note**
>
> *Every time you begin the wonky cut, the center strips of the block need to be horizontal if cutting right-handed and vertical if left-handed.*

1. Place the marked square ruler at an angle, so that the corners of the 10½″ × 10½″ marked square touch each edge of the block and the center of the square (5¼″ mark) is directly over the center seam (page 11). Notice the difference from the ruler angle for Block A. Trim.

Left-handed	Right-handed

Correct ruler angle for first 2 cuts of Block B

2. Rotate the block and square the other 2 sides of the block to measure 10½″ × 10½″ (page 12). Make the following number of blocks:

Crib: 6   Lap: 10   Twin: 12   Queen: 24   King: 32

Block B

QUILT CONSTRUCTION

1. Place the blocks in rows, alternating the A and B blocks.

2. Sew the blocks into rows, alternating the pressing direction of the seams. Press the seams to the right in the first row, to the left in the second row, to the right in the third row, and so on.

3. Sew the rows together, matching the seams.

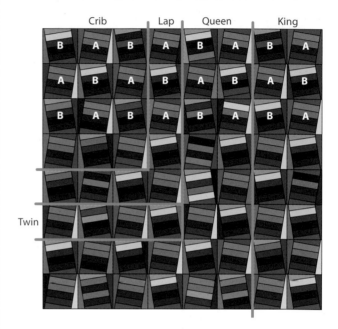

BORDERS

It's time to grab those border strips we cut earlier.

This quilt has 4 borders. Border 2 has several options; choose which option you like best from Options for Border 2 (pages 61–63).

See General Border Instructions (page 60) to measure correct border lengths. None of us sews an exact ¼″ seam. Some of us sew a generous ¼″ and our quilt tops are smaller than the quilt tops of those of us who sew scant ¼″ seams. For this reason it is always a good idea to measure your quilt to get the correct border strip length needed every time you add a border.

See Bodacious Border Techniques and Options (pages 60–63) for complete sewing instructions for all borders.

	CRIB	LAP	TWIN	QUEEN	KING
Border 1	2 strips 1½″ × 30½″ 2 strips 1½″ × 42½″	2 strips 2″ × 40½″ 2 strips 2″ × 62½″	2 strips 2″ × 40½″ 2 strips 2″ × 63½″	2 strips 2″ × 60½″ 2 strips 2″ × 83½″	2 strips 2″ × 80½″ 2 strips 2″ × 83½″
Border 2	2 strips 2½″ × 32½″ 2 strips 2½″ × 46½″	2 strips 3½″ × 40½″ (top and bottom only)	2 strips 3½″ × 43½″ 2 strips 3½″ × 69½″	2 strips 3½″ × 63½″ 2 strips 3½″ × 89½″	2 strips 3½″ × 83½″ 2 strips 3½″ × 89½″
Border 3	2 strips 1½″ × 36½″ 2 strips 1½″ × 48½″	2 strips 2″ × 40½″ (top and bottom only)	2 strips 2″ × 49½″ 2 strips 2″ × 72½″	2 strips 2″ × 69½″ 2 strips 2″ × 92½″	2 strips 2″ × 89½″ 2 strips 2″ × 92½″
Border 4	2 strips 3½″ × 38½″ 2 strips 3½″ × 54½″	2 strips 6½″ × 43½″ 2 strips 6½″ × 74½″	2 strips 6½″ × 52½″ 2 strips 6½″ × 84½″	2 strips 8½″ × 72½″ 2 strips 8½″ × 108½″	2 strips 8½″ × 92½″ 2 strips 8½″ × 108½″

Boardwalk II, 55″ × 74″
Quilt made by Judy Hugo
and quilted by Nancy Frank.
Border 2 uses options 3 and 4 (pages 62 and 63).

Borders can be playful and involve more than just the edges of the quilt top. A border is a great place to use up scraps left over from the piecing process. Using the scraps in the border ties everything together and makes for an interesting, exciting, and eye-catching finish.

For each quilt in this book I've added a total of four borders. Border 2 can include optional piecing. This is where you can use up all those scraps you have left on your cutting mat. There are several options for how to do this.

GENERAL BORDER INSTRUCTIONS

1. When determining the size of the quilt and the length needed for borders, always measure through the center of the quilt, not along the sides.

2. Sew on the top and bottom borders first. Measure across the center of the quilt, and then cut and piece border strips as needed to achieve the length required for the width of the quilt.

3. Mark the center of the border strip and the center of the quilt on the edge that you are going to sew the border to.

4. With right sides together, line up the marks on the border strip and the quilt, and pin in the center and at the ends. Then continue to pin from the center to the corner along each edge of the quilt, so that when you are done you have pins along the whole edge, easing in any extra fabric there may be. I encourage you to use lots of pins.

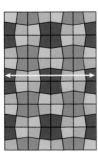
Measure horizontally.

Add top and bottom borders.

5. Use a ¼˝ seam allowance and press the border seams out or open.

6. It is important to measure each time you add a border. Measure the length of the quilt top through the center, including the new borders. Piece any strips end to end as needed as you did for the top and bottom.

7. Sew the side borders on as you did for the top and bottom.

8. Press. The rule of thumb is to press the seams away from the center of the quilt top or press them open.

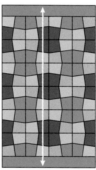
Measure vertically.

Add side borders.

*TIPS

■ If you have to ease fabric to make it all fit, place the side that has to be eased (the side that has the longer piece of fabric) on the machine bed. The presser foot will push the fabric on top and the feed dogs hold the fabric on the bottom, helping even out the way the fabric lies together.

■ Sew on the top and bottom borders first, and then the sides. The eye unconsciously registers the sewn seam, so having a vertical seam gives the impression of a longer quilt. If you sew the side borders on first, the eye registers the horizontal seam, giving a shorter/wider impression.

LAP QUILT

This quilt uses Borders 1, 2 (see options at right), and 3 on the top and bottom only and Borders 1 and 4 on the sides.

1. Sew Borders 1, 2, and 3 to the top and bottom.

2. Sew Border 1 to the sides.

3. Sew Border 4 to the top and bottom and then to the sides.

Borders 1, 2, and 3 on top and bottom

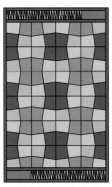

Border 1 on sides

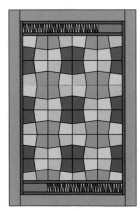

Border 4

OPTIONS FOR BORDER 2

Option 1

This is the simplest border option.

All four sides have the same fabric. No fancy piecing is required. Follow the directions (page 60) for sewing on borders.

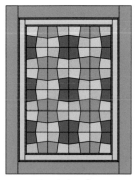

Simple borders

Border detail of *Flights of Fancy II* (page 29)

Option 2

The inner border (Border 1) is sewn exactly the same way as in option 1, and then you add some interesting shapes to Border 2 using a very easy rough-edge appliqué technique.

1. From your scraps, cut shapes that you think will enhance the quilt. In *Bejeweled* (page 36), I used diamonds in Border 2.

2. Sew on all the borders, following the steps in the general instructions (page 60).

3. Once all the borders are sewn on, hang the quilt on a design wall (or place it on the floor) and place the shapes wherever you like them.

Border detail of *Bejeweled* (page 36)

Raw-Edge Appliqué—The Technique

1. Cut any shapes you'd like to have in the border.

2. Using a fabric basting glue (I like to use Roxanne Glue Baste-It) on the wrong side of the fabric, dab glue along the edge, and then position and stick the shape in place.

3. With the sewing machine set on a straight stitch, stitch along the edge of the shape.

4. When quilting the quilt, quilt right over the appliquéd shapes, thus ensuring that they'll stay put over time.

Option 3

This option uses the larger scraps that have been left over from cutting strips.

1. Cut pieces the width of the border (Crib: 2½˝; All other sizes: 3½˝) and any length.

2. Piece these strips together to make the length needed. You can sew them together with 45° or straight seams. These pieced strips don't have to go all around the quilt; they can be used as only a portion of the border.

3. Follow the General Border Instructions (page 60) for sewing on the pieced border strips.

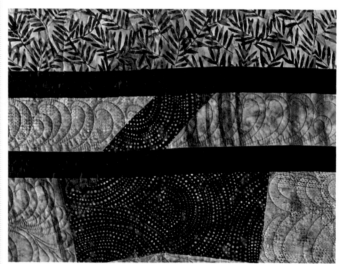

Border detail of *Stepping Stones* (page 13)

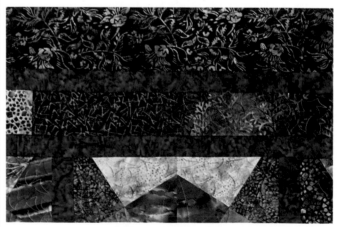

Border detail of *Whimsy* (page 48)

Option 4

With this option, you use those pointy pieces of fabric you have left over from the wonky cutting.

1. Sew the points together, alternating the wide and narrow ends.

2. Sew enough together to make an 8″ long piece, and then trim to the width you want (Crib: 2½″; All other sizes: 3½″).

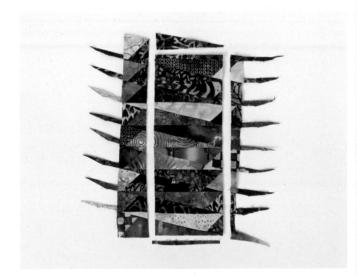

3. Make as many as you want or can, and then sew the 8″ strips together to make the length you want to be included in the border. There will not be enough to go around the entire quilt. This really is just to add some spark—a little eye-catching accent—to the border.

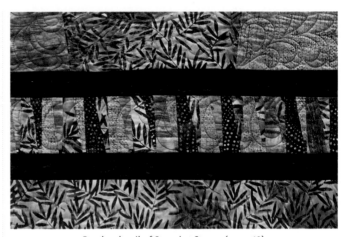

Border detail of *Stepping Stones* (page 13)

Border detail of *Nine-Patch Passion* (page 30)

Border detail of *Squared Away* (page 42)

ABOUT THE AUTHOR

Born in Singapore to Dutch parents, Marlous lived in the United Kingdom and traveled the globe before emigrating to the United States. She has always had a love of color, texture, and design, and while studying Japanese and art history in college she had the opportunity to explore several art media—pottery, soft sculpture, mosaic, painting, and costume design. It was only much later that she discovered her passion for quilting.

She has been quilting in earnest for about ten years. Always wishing to "make things her own," she was never one to follow a pattern from start to finish, as written. At the urging of family and friends, she created Marlous Designs, a small unique quilt pattern company. Marlous has enjoyed success as a quilt designer with the help of her friend Judy Hugo.

Marlous lives in New York, in a small town in the foothills of the Adirondacks, with her extremely supportive husband. They have two grown sons who are always vying to get first dibs on a new quilt. She works part-time at a local quilt shop, Gloversville Sewing Center, where her boss, co-workers, and customers constantly give creative advice, ideas, and support.

Great Titles *from* C&T PUBLISHING

Available at your local retailer or **www.ctpub.com** *or* **800-284-1114**

For a list of other fine books from C&T Publishing, visit our website to view our catalog online.

C&T PUBLISHING, INC.
P.O. Box 1456
Lafayette, CA 94549
800-284-1114

Email: ctinfo@ctpub.com
Website: www.ctpub.com

C&T Publishing's professional photography services are now available to the public. Visit us at www.ctmediaservices.com.

Tips and Techniques can be found at www.ctpub.com > Consumer Resources > Quiltmaking Basics: Tips & Techniques for Quiltmaking & More

For quilting supplies:

COTTON PATCH
1025 Brown Ave.
Lafayette, CA 94549
Store: 925-284-1177
Mail order: 925-283-7883

Email: CottonPa@aol.com
Website: www.quiltusa.com

Note: Fabrics used in the quilts shown may not be currently available, as fabric manufacturers keep most fabrics in print for only a short time.